D.D. HOME

D.D. HOME
The Man Who Talked with Ghosts

I.G. EDMONDS

publishers since 1798

THOMAS NELSON INC., PUBLISHERS
Nashville   New York

First edition

Library of Congress Cataloging in Publication Data

Edmonds, I   G
   D. D. Home: the man who talked with ghosts.

   Bibliography: p. 181
   BF1283.H7E35   133.9′1′0924   [B]   78–7579
   1.   Home, Daniel Dunglas, 1833–1886.   2.   Mediums—
Great Britain—Biography.   I.   Title.
BF1283.H7E35   133.9w1w0924   [B]   78–7579
ISBN 0–8407–6584–3

CONTENTS

D.D. HOME

Daniel Dunglas Home as he appeared in 1855 soon after his arrival in England. He was then twenty-two years old.

1

TRUE MEDIUM OR CLEVER FRAUD?

Daniel Dunglas Home claimed that he could talk with ghosts. These spirits, he said, were his friends. In addition to communicating with him through mysterious spirit rapping, they aided Home in doing peculiar tricks. Once they assisted him in floating out the window of a three-story house and back in another window. They also protected him when he put his head in a blazing fireplace. He could pick up red-hot coals in his hand and cause tables and chairs to move across the room, apparently untouched except by the hands of his spirit friends.

In doing such unusual things, Home naturally opened himself to the charge of being a fraud. He was a spiritualist medium at a time when thousands of "spook crooks" were robbing the gullible by claiming to be able to communicate with the dead. Home was unique among these mediums. He never accepted money for his work. Where others hid their trickery in total darkness, Home worked—except on rare occasions—in some sort of light. His guests were invited to interrupt at any time to search for hidden conjurer's apparatus. They often did, but nothing was ever found. Unlike the other famous mediums of his day, no one ever proved that Home used trickery of any sort.

Home's feats sound fantastic and impossible as we read of them today, more than 100 years later. However, the testimony of those who saw him is impressive. Even more impressive are the names of the people who believed in Home's ability to talk with ghosts.

There is William Cullen Bryant, the American poet. Napoleon III of France, an amateur magician, believed that Home used tricks of stage magic—until he met this strange man. His Majesty then became a believer. Elizabeth Barrett Browning, the English poetess, believed ardently in Home. Edward Bulwer-Lytton, author of *The Last Days of Pompeii*, believed and later used Home as the model for a character in a book called *A Strange Story*. Alexandre Dumas, author of *The Three Musketeers*, believed in Home. Sir William Crookes, one of the most noted scientists of his day, put Home in a wire cage to isolate the medium for scientific investigations of Home's occult powers. Czar Alexander II of Russia was another believer, and so was Arthur Conan Doyle, creator of Sherlock Homes.

On the other hand, Charles Dickens did not believe in Home. Robert Browning, the English poet, hated Home so much that he threatened to kill the medium if they met again. He denounced William Makepeace Thackeray, author of *Vanity Fair*, for publicly supporting Home. Nathaniel Hawthorne, the famous American author, did not give his own opinion of Home, but confessed that Browning bored him by talking about Home so much. The noted scientist Sir David Brewster was vicious in his denunciation of Home.

And so it went. It is important to remember, however, that not one of Home's enemies was able to prove him a fake. Houdini, the world-famous American magician, claimed that he could duplicate any of Home's feats through regular stage magic. However, when challenged to do so by floating out a window and back in an adjoining window three stories from the ground—*in the same house and under the same conditions as Home's*—Houdini failed to go through with his demonstration.

So the question still remains: Was Daniel Dunglas Home a man who really had ghostly friends, or was he the world's best faker? No one has been able to prove either statement. But regardless of whether he was a true medium or a clever fraud, the life of Daniel Dunglas Home is very unusual. From a penniless youth in Connecticut Home went on his way until in the end he walked with kings and queens.

In the chapters that follow I have reported Home's feats as described by those who saw them. I have done this in most cases without comment on how they might have been done by trickery. Then in the final chapter of the book I have described methods by which a modern magician could duplicate most of them. However, there are many ways of doing any trick, and there is no guarantee that this is what Home did. But one thing is certain: He either used methods something like those described, or he really did have helpful ghostly friends.

2

THE FLOATING MAN

There were five men on the third floor of the London mansion belonging to young Lord Lindsay. In addition to the host, there were John Lord Adare, Captain Charles Wynne, and Captain Gerald Smith. The four were tense and expectant as they watched the fifth man in the room. He was Daniel Dunglas Home, a young Scotsman who had grown up in the United States. Home was slumped in a chair, his chin on his chest. He had fallen into a trance.

Lindsay looked around at Lord Adare, his face mirroring his uneasiness. He started to speak, but Adare shook his head. They both turned back to stare at the quiet form of their companion.

There was only a single small candle in the room. This in itself was unusual, for Home preferred—unlike most spiritualists—to work in the presence of at least some light, so that no one could accuse him of trickery.

All four men had seen strange things happen in Home's presence. During a previous séance, a chair had moved across the room. A table rose up in the air. The witnesses had quickly looked underneath to see how he had pushed it up, but found nothing. Strange raps had tapped out messages supposedly from men long dead. These mysterious sounds had seemed to come from different parts of the room, all far removed from Home. Tonight, however, he had promised them something entirely different. They waited, both expectant and uneasy.

The suspense built up as Home continued to slump in his chair. Then suddenly—with a movement so unexpected that it startled the men watching him—Home leaped to his feet. He was about five feet ten in height, slender but well built. His auburn hair was well groomed. His face was slightly effeminate and dead white, and his eyes were a light blue. They appeared very mild in the daytime, but those who knew him said they took on a rather strange glitter at night. The somewhat effeminate features were improved by a drooping moustache, then in fashion among young men. All in all, Daniel Home looked more like the public conception of a poet than like one of the most mysterious men of his time.

Home turned away from his companions. His eyes were staring, and he walked somewhat jerkily as he left the room. The four witnesses did not follow. Earlier Home had warned them not to leave their seats. Any movement by them could break his spell. "This," he told them, "would put me in grave danger."

Listening intently, they could hear Home's footsteps crossing the adjoining room, then the sound of a window being raised.

Lindsay shifted uncertainly in his seat. He looked around at Lord Adare. "In his condition—" he began.

A wave of Adare's had silenced him. "Any interference now could be more dangerous than anything he might do to himself," he whispered. "I have implicit faith in Dan."

Lindsay looked very unhappy. After all, it was his house. If a guest fell out the window and killed himself, it would look bad for him. At that moment, Lord Adare gasped. Lindsay and the two army officers looked around. They saw Adare with a stunned expression pointing with a trembling finger toward the window of their room. The window was closed, but beyond it they saw Home. The medium was apparently standing on air outside the window. The ground was three stories below. As they sat gripped in an occult thrill, Home opened the window and stepped into the room. He crossed the room, still in a trance, and took his original position in the chair.

Suddenly Home laughed softly. Captain Wynne asked what he was laughing at. Home replied in a flat, curious voice rather unlike his normal tones: "I was thinking how astonished a policeman would have been if he had looked up and seen me floating between the windows!"

He was obviously still in his trance. He appeared calm, but when he came out of the trance a short time later, he was greatly agitated. He trembled slightly. He made no reference to his strange experience, but muttered something about feeling himself in danger.

In describing the event to his father, the Earl of Dunraven, Lord Adare wrote:

> Home remained in a highly nervous condition for a short time. Then gradually he became quiet. . . .
> We then had a series of curious manifestations.

Lindsay and Charlie [Wynne] saw tongues or jets of flame proceeding from Home's head. We then all distinctly heard, as it were, a bird flying around the room. It was whistling and chirping. But we saw nothing; except Lindsay, who perceived an indistinct form resembling a bird.

There then came the sound of a great wind rushing through the room. The moaning, rushing sound was the most weird thing I have ever heard.

After the séance, at Home's request, the four men inspected the windows to assure themselves that no wires or framework had been placed outside to help him between the windows. They found nothing.

Later Wynne and Adare discussed the strange evening in great detail. They completely discounted the possibility of trickery. As Adare pointed out, Home had never been in Lindsay's house before. He arrived in the company of Adare and had never left his friend's presence. Therefore it was impossible for him to have placed any mechanical aids in the room or outside on the wall. He could not have employed an accomplice because none of them but Lindsay knew which room they would occupy. Home had requested this.

This happened in 1868. In 1870, the Earl of Dunraven, Lord Adare's father, had his son's letter about the séance printed in a book along with other letters regarding Home's extraordinary actions. Years later, Adare said that he had been a very young man when he wrote these letters. However, he added, the passing years had not caused him to change his mind about Home. He felt that the Scotsman was indeed in touch with the occult.

In 1868 Adare was a rich young sportsman with a deep interest in the supernatural. It has been suggested that the four young men were overly subject to suggestion, and also, in the manner of young blades of the time, possibly half-drunk as well. There is no proof of this. However, if one chooses to discount Adare's testimony, there are many other people who testified to Home's apparently supernatural gifts.

One of those who supported him was Princess Metternich, whose husband was an Austrian diplomat. In 1863, in Paris, Madame Jauvin d'Attainville was giving a party for the Metternichs. Prince Joachim Murat asked if he could bring his house guest, Daniel Dunglas Home.

Madame d'Attainville was annoyed at the prince. Home was well known in Paris by that time, and some of the amazing things he had done had come back to Madame in a garbled form. Prince Murat quickly explained that Home was not a professional entertainer—he was a gentleman. He refused to take money; he never gave a séance for a stranger; he insisted upon being properly introduced. Then he would only perform as an invited guest on an equal status with the other guests. He had an occult gift which he was willing to share with his friends and with no others. Prince Murat mentioned a few highly placed names that Home had turned down.

The prince neglected to mention that though Home refused pay for his séances, he was delighted to receive expensive thank-you gifts. He especially loved gifts of jewelry, which he treasured. Even in his most poverty-stricken days, he refused to sell a single piece. They were both treasures and a journal of his life. In later years he could tell those who inquired the complete history of each jewel—who gave it to him, where, and what the occasion was.

Madame d'Attainville was sufficiently impressed to include Home in her invitation list for the party. As usual, Home created intense interest among the guests. He promised to call his friends the spirits after dinner— if the spirits were agreeable. He went on to explain to the guests, as he always did, that he had no control over the spirits. He did not employ magic and was not a wizard. The spirits came only if they chose to do so.

Fortunately, this was a night the spirits chose to make contact with their friend, D. D. Home. It is also fortunate that Princess Pauline Metternich recorded the evening in her memoirs, *The Days That Are No More.*

After dinner the guests moved to a spacious drawing room. They were seated around a large table directly under a chandelier that cast a bright light over the entire room. Home did not sit at the table with the guests. He took a chair back from the others. Although he did not comment on it, this was done to allay any suspicions that he was working some mechanical apparatus under the table by using his feet. Several fake mediums had recently been exposed for doing just this.

As usual, Home slumped in his chair and went into a trance. There was a deep silence in the room. Both doubters and believers in spiritualism waited in suspense for the first appearance of Home's ghostly friends. The doubters were actually more eager than the believers, for they hoped to gain notoriety by exposing the famous man.

Suddenly there were rapping noises. Prince Metternich, one of the doubters, noted with surprise that none of the noises came from the vicinity of the medium. The sounds came from the walls, the ceiling, and from under the table at which the guests sat.

Home sat up straight in his chair, although his blank, trancelike expression did not change. "Is that you, Bryan?" he asked. He had previously explained that

Bryan was his most reliable spirit friend. Home was answered by another knock and then several others. The medium said in a loud voice: *"They* are all about us!"

The guests had to take his word for it. They could see nothing. The strange rapping noises became louder and more frequent. Some of the more sensitive guests whispered that they actually felt the touch of invisible hands. Prince Metternich thought this was caused by overactive imaginations.

The ghostly rappings were only the curtain raiser for a real shock. The tablecloth covering the table at which the guests sat started to rise in the center. The startled viewers thought they could see the impression of a hand apparently pushing from underneath the cloth. This was clearly impossible, for the hand would have had to pass through the solid-mahogany tabletop.

One of the male guests jumped to his feet, grabbed the edge of the cloth, and jerked it from the table. There was *nothing* under the cloth. Prince Metternich dropped to his knees to look under the table. He also found nothing. He resumed his seat with a baffled expression.

Home, in his trance, gave no indication that he observed these attempts to catch him in some trickery. He had earlier urged them to do so if they could.

The doubters now watched the proceedings with more serious faces. They still disbelieved in Home's occult powers, but they no longer thought that exposing him would be easy. They were also baffled by the bright light from the overhead chandelier that made Home's every movement clear to them.

Next, a bouquet of flowers floated serenely across the room with no visible means of support. It dropped lightly into Princess Metternich's lap. Before she could pick them up, her husband grabbed the flowers. The prince knew a little something about magic through his acquaintance with the famous magician Robert-Houdin, who had a theater in Paris. He knew that magicians made cards and small articles float by attaching a thin black thread to them. This thread cannot be seen by the audience. However, the prince found no thread, wires, or anything else that could account for the strange movement of the bouquet.

The party broke up soon after this. The guests left, talking among themselves of the wonders they had seen and heard. Some were still not convinced, but all were honest enough to admit that they had no idea how Home had accomplished his tricks.

The important question that intrigued even those who were disbelievers were how Home could have arranged any deception in a strange house he had never entered before. Madame d'Attainville was positive that none of her servants could have helped him in any deception. Then how had he fooled them?

One argument used by Home's supporters was that he was too much of a gentleman to stoop to deception. And his bearing was that of a gentleman. All agreed his deportment and manners were perfect. His only character defect—if indeed it can be called such—was a snobbish hunger to move in the circles of the royal and the famous.

This was quite an ambition for a penniless young man, the son of a carpenter, who had been born in a small Scottish village. However, the Home family (whose original name was Hume) descended from an illegitimate son of the famous Humes of Dunglass. As a result Daniel considered himself of aristocratic blood.

He saw no reason whatsoever why he should not use his strange occult ability to converse with the dead to live like an aristocrat himself.

And he did, from the time he set out on his occult career at the age of seventeen until he died in Paris, France, at the age of fifty-three.

3

THE CHILD
SPIRITUALISTS

Daniel Dunglas Home was born in a little village near Edinburgh, Scotland, on March 20, 1833. In his autobiography, *Incidents in My Life,* Home says practically nothing about his father. But of his mother, he said:

My mother was a seer throughout her life. She had what is known in Scotland as second sight. In many instances she saw things which were afterwards found to have occurred at a distance, just as she had described them. She also foretold many events which occurred in the family, and foretold the passing away of relatives. And, lastly, she foretold her own [death] four months before it happened.

Mrs. Home was born Betsey McNeal. Several members of the McNeal family were also said to be seers. She was connected with the Mackenzie family, which produced the famous seventeenth-century mystic known as the Brahan Seer.

23

Kenneth Mackenzie, the Brahan Seer, gained an enormous reputation in Scotland for his amazingly accurate gift of prophecy. He then angered the Countess of Seaforth with one of his prophecies. She had him put to death in revenge. Before he died, Mackenzie "drew forth his white stone, so long the instrument of his supernatural intelligence. Once more applying his eye to it, he said, "I see into the far future, and I read the doom of the race of my oppressor." He then prophesied the final extinction of the Seaforth family in a manner that came true in complete detail.

Daniel, apparently, inherited both the McNeal and the Mackenzie occult powers. This power began to show itself very early. When he was one year old, Daniel was adopted by his mother's sister, Mary McNeal Cook. Home wrote that he could not remember when his occult powers first appeared, but "my aunt and others have told me that when I was a baby my cradle was frequently rocked, as if some kind guardian spirit was tending me in my slumbers."

Another story he heard from his aunt was how he foretold the death of a small cousin. He was then four years old. However, the first occult vision that Daniel could recall in later life happened when he was thirteen.

Daniel had a tendency toward tuberculosis and was quite frail in those years. He could not engage in the strenuous sports of other boys his age. In his loneliness he took long walks in the woods, taking pleasure in the beauties of nature. When he tired, he would sit under a tree and read a small Bible he carried with him.

He was fortunate in meeting a fifteen-year-old boy who shared his interests. "We were in the habit of reading the Bible together," Home wrote in his memoirs. "Upon one occasion, in the month of April, we had been reading it in the woods. We were both of us silently contemplating the beauties of the springtime vegetation, when he turned to me and said, 'I have been reading such a strange story!' "

It proved to be a ghost story. They discussed the story. "We then agreed," Home said, "that whichever one of us should be first called from earth, would, if God permitted it, appear to the other the third day afterwards."

At that time the Cook family was living in Connecticut in the United States, having moved there from Scotland when Daniel was nine. Soon after Daniel and his friend made their pact, the friend, Edwin, moved to Troy, New York.

In June, just as Daniel was preparing to go to bed, his bedroom suddenly got very dark, although the moon was shining brightly outside. The darkness increased in the room. Then, according to Home's memoirs:

Through the darkness there seemed to be a gleam of light, which I cannot describe. But it seemed similar to those which I and others have since seen when the room has been illuminated by spiritual presence. The light increased. My attention was drawn to the foot of my bed, where stood my friend Edwin.

He appeared as a cloud of brightness, illumining his face with a distinctness more than mortal. . . . He looked on me with a smile of ineffable sweetness. Then slowly raising his right arm, he pointed upward, and making with it three circles in the air. The hand began slowly to disappear and then the arm, and finally the whole body melted away.

I was speechless and could not move. As soon as the power of movement was restored, I rang the bell. The family, thinking I was ill, came to my room. I cried, 'I have seen Edwin—he died three days ago at this very hour!' "

His aunt accused him of having hallucinations, but a few days later they received a letter saying that Edwin had died exactly on the date and at the time Daniel had envisioned.

Two years later, when Daniel was fifteen, the famous Hydesville Mystery created a national sensation. This unusual event ushered in the era of modern spiritualism.

Mankind, of course, had believed in ghosts and spirits as far back as history and anthropology can take us. At first primitive man believed that spirits lived in all things. There were spirits in rocks, trees, water, fire, and such. These spirits had power of both good and evil. Mankind could ask their help and try to bribe them with offerings and prayer. Later the idea of magic developed. Men thought that they could control spirits through the use of magical formulas and incantations. Ghosts could come back, especially the ghosts of those who had died violent deaths. Many spirits could not rest in their graves because they had not been avenged. Tales of haunted houses and ghosts were told by the thousands.

But all these ghosts were fearful and uncontrollable by man. Spiritualism envisioned a happy world of ghosts beyond human sight. These spirits could communicate with people through *mediums*. Mediums are men, women, or children who supposedly have a special occult gift that permits them to receive communications from friendly spirits.

Spiritualism, of course, had been in existence before the famous Hydesville Mystery, but it was this curious experience involving two young girls that started the national and later international craze for talking with the dead.

It began in the home of a farmer named John D. Fox in March 1848. The family was awakened by bumping noises they could not explain. Later Margaret Fox, John Fox's wife, signed a statement telling what happened:

> On the night of the first disturbance we got up, lighted a candle and searched the entire house. . . . Although not very loud, it produced a jar on the bedsteads and chairs that could be felt when we were in bed. We could feel the jar when standing on the floor. It continued on this night until we slept.

The noises returned on March 30, 1848, continuing all night:

> The noises were heard in all parts of the house. . . . We heard footsteps in the pantry, and walking upstairs. We could not rest. I then concluded that the house must be haunted by some unhappy restless spirit. I had often heard of such things, but had never witnessed anything of the kind that I could not account for.

The following night, March 31, there occurred the event that started the spiritualism craze. Mr. and Mrs. Fox moved the bed of their daughters, Margaretta and Catharine (Katie), into their own room after the mysterious knocking started. They had just gone to bed when the noise started again. According to Congressman Robert Dale Owen, who interviewed both Mrs. Fox and her two daughters, it was a windy night. John Fox thought the noise might be coming from window sashes rattling in the wind. He went to the window and began trying to shake the sashes.

Suddenly eleven-year-old Katie noticed that each time her father rattled the window, the knocks seemed

28

Modern spiritualism began with the mysterious
rappings heard and answered by the Fox sisters:
Margaretta, left, Katie, center, and Leah.

to answer. She snapped her fingers, crying to her sister's
astonishment: "Here, Mr. Splitfoot [meaning the Devil],
do as I do!" The knocks immediately echoed the snap of
her fingers! Katie was so frightened that she ducked her
head under the bedcovers.

Her fourteen-year-old sister, Margaretta, took up the
challenge. She said, "Do just as I do!" She clapped her

hands together four times. Instantly there were four hollow raps from the opposite wall.

By this time Katie Fox had recovered her courage. She threw back the covers, crying to her mother: "Tomorrow is April Fool's Day! Someone is trying to trick us!"

Mrs. Fox did not agree. Nervously she asked the unknown rapper to knock out the ages of her children. Immediately there were fourteen raps, which was Margaretta's age. There was a pause. Then eleven raps followed. This was Katie's age.

Mrs. Fox was now sure that some intelligence was behind the strange rappings. The family's initial fear had subsided. The ghostly rapper seemed to mean them no harm. It apparently only wanted to communicate with them.

"Are you a spirit?" Mrs. Fox asked. "If so, make two raps."

Two rapping sounds immediately came from the wall. She took a deep nervous breath and continued her questions. They learned that the spirit was a man of thirty-two years. He had been murdered in the house at some time before the Fox family moved in. Mrs. Fox asked if she could call in her neighbors to hear the raps. The spirit replied with two raps, the signal they had agreed on for yes.

A number of neighbors came in response to her call. Some were incredulous, refusing to believe they were not being tricked. Others accepted the noise as coming from a real spirit. Some of the believers joined John Fox the next day in digging in the cellar, where the rapper said his body had been buried. They soon struck water. It seeped into the hole, making it impossible to dig any deeper.

Visitors continued to flock to the house to hear the strange raps. According to Mrs. Fox, at one time there were as many as three hundred people either in the house or waiting to get in. The mystery was compounded later in the year, when further digging in the cellar revealed a plank, some ashes, quicklime, and what appeared to be some human hair and one bone.

Word of the Hydesville Mystery swept across the nation as newspapers printed the sensational story. Katie and Margaretta, urged on by their older sister, Leah Fox Fish, began public séances in which they supposedly made contact with spirits who rapped out their answers.

Thousands came and believed. Many others denounced the girls as fakes. One newspaper branded their séances as "Spiritualist Humbug." Once a committee of suspicious women tied the girls' hands and feet, and then challenged them to produce their raps. The girls were frightened by the angry women, and Katie broke into tears. Then the rappings broke out, louder than ever, convincing the women that they did not come from the girls. Another time a mob of antispiritualists broke into a séance hall and threatened to lynch the frightened girls as accomplices of the devil.

The enormous publicity given to the Hydesville Mystery convinced others that they could also converse with ghosts. Hundreds announced themselves as mediums. Daniel Home was fifteen years old at the time. In later years he claimed he only vaguely heard of the Fox sisters, but knew nothing of their work. It does not seem possible that he could really have been in ignorance of such a startling thing as the apparent ability of ordinary people to communicate with the dead.

If Home was indeed indifferent to the sensational news, two young brothers in Buffalo, New York, were not. Nine-year-old Ira Davenport and his seven-year-old brother, William Henry Davenport, were enraptured by the stories of two young girls who could talk with ghosts. They immediately tried to do the same. In time they grew up to be the famous Davenport brothers, whose path would cross Home's years later in London, England.

4

DANCING TABLES
AND AN ANGRY AUNT

After seeing the spirit of his dead friend Edwin, Daniel began to experience increasing contact with the occult. At the same time he turned more and more toward religion. He did not care for the stern Scottish Presbyterianism of his Aunt Mary. Instead he went to the Methodist church. This infuriated Mrs. Cook, who could not "abide those Wesleyans!" He then joined the Congregationalist church.

Four years had now passed since he saw Edwin's ghost and two years since the strange rapping at the Fox home started the spiritualism craze. The Fox sisters had become professional mediums, and hundreds of others were claiming to be mediums also. Events were shaping up that would cause Daniel to join in the movement.

In the spring of 1850, when Daniel was seventeen, he was living in Norwich, Connecticut. His mother had recently moved to Waterford, a town about twelve miles away. One day Daniel felt a strong impression that his mother wanted him badly. He immediately took leave of his aunt and walked the twelve miles to see Mrs. Home.

He greeted her with the words, "What have you to say to me, Mother?"

"Well, dear, it is only to tell you that four months from this time, I shall leave you," Mrs. Home replied.

In his autobiography Home wrote: "I asked incredulously how she knew, and she said, 'Your little sister Mary [who had died four years previously] came to me in a vision. She held four lilies in her hand. She allowed them to slip from her fingers one after the other. When the last one fell, she said, 'And then you will come to me.' "

Mrs. Home also told Daniel that none of her family would be present "to close my eyes."

Four months later to the day, Daniel, back at his Aunt Mary's, was awakened in the night by a voice that said, "Midnight, Daniel."

He sprang up and saw his mother near the window. She repeated the words "twelve o'clock" twice and disappeared. Daniel, in great agitation, called Mrs. Cook. When she came, he said, "Aunty, Mother died at twelve o'clock!"

Mrs. Cook had little sympathy for second sight. She crossly told the boy that he was dreaming and to go back to sleep. Then the next day she was stunned to receive word that her sister had died at twelve o'clock. Even more startling, her death came while visiting friends. So there had been no members of her family present "to close my eyes," as she had predicted to Daniel four months before.

A short time after this, Daniel was eating breakfast when rapping noises began to sound from the table. They resembled similar noises he had heard in his bedroom the night before. He thought then that the raps might have come from creakings of the old house, but these strange noises from the breakfast table could not be so easily explained away.

Mrs. Cook turned pale. She cried, "You have brought the devil to my house!"

A staunch believer that the Kirk (Church) of Scotland was the only true religious order, the deeply religious woman was convinced that the "devil's raps" were caused by her nephew's joining another congregation.

In his autobiography Home says of this incident: "I ought to say here that there had then been some talk of the so-called Rochester knocking through the Fox family, but apart from casually hearing of them, I had paid no attention to them. I did not know even what they meant." (Since Hydesville was close to Rochester, many newspapers had reported the Fox story as the Rochester Mystery.)

For a person who had been psychic since early childhood, it seems very unusual that Daniel would not have been intrigued and thrilled by the unusual stories of the Fox sisters' supposed contact with the dead. However, except for two periods of his life, he always shunned other mediums and tried to give the impression that he had learned nothing from any of them. Unlikely or not, that is his claim.

"My aunt, on the contrary, had heard of the Rochester knockings from some of the neighbors," Home wrote. "She considered them as some works of the Evil One. In her uncontrolled anger, she seized a chair and threw it at me."

Mrs. Cook was not one to be daunted by the devil. Declaring war on the mysterious source of the rappings, she sought religious help. According to Daniel:

There were in the village three ministers, one a Congregationalist, one a Baptist, and the other a Wesleyan. In the afternoon, my aunt, her anger having for the moment caused her to lose sight of her prejudices against these rival persuasions, sent for them to consult with her, and to pray for me, that I might be freed from these visitations.

This had exactly the opposite effect upon young Daniel. He came away from his sessions with the ministers more strongly convinced than ever that he had a God-given gift. This came about during his visit with the Baptist minister summoned by his aunt. The cleric, the Reverend Mr. Mussey, suggested that they pray together that the strange rapping should cease. Home reported:

> Whilst we were thus engaged in prayer, at every mention of the Holy names of God or Jesus, there came gentle raps on the minister's chair and in different parts of the room.
>
> I was so struck, and so impressed by this, that there and then upon my knees, I resolved to follow the leadings of that which I then felt must be good and true, else why should it have signified its joy at those special portions of the prayer?

He went on to say that this was the turning point of his life. The Methodist minister called by his aunt insisted that talking with spirits was wicked. Daniel was disturbed by this but felt better when the minister explained that this applied to those who call up spirits. Daniel claimed that he had never called for any spirits. In fact, he did not even know how. Every time one had appeared to him, as in the case of his friend Edwin and his mother, it had come unbidden. It was the same with the mysterious spirit rappings. The spirits themselves decided when they would make themselves known to him.

For the rest of his life Daniel maintained this claim. At different periods, the power to communicate with his spirits left him, withdrawn for a time because, he assumed, he had somehow offended them. This is one of the things that set Daniel Home apart from his fellow mediums of the mid-nineteenth century. They claimed the ability to contact ghosts. Home claimed that spirits contacted him and only when they chose to do so.

After his meeting with the three ministers, Daniel Home began to experience still stranger manifestations:

> Furniture began to move about without any visible agency. The first time this occurred I was in my room brushing my hair before the looking-glass. In the glass I saw a chair moving slowly toward me. My first feeling was one of intense fear. When within about a foot of me it stopped. Whereupon I jumped past it, and rushed down stairs.

Later in the living room with his aunt and uncle, Home was again startled by self-moving furniture. When a heavy table started dancing about, Mrs. Cook brought the family Bible and placed it on the table.

"There!" she cried. "That will drive the devils away!"

Home reports, "To her astonishment the table only moved in a more lively manner, as if pleased to bear such a burden."

This strange experience strengthened Home's belief that there was nothing sinister or evil in these spirit actions, otherwise, the influence of the Bible would have counteracted them. Still further support came from his mother's spirit. While visiting another aunt, who was not as bitterly opposed to spirits as Mrs. Cook, Home got this message from his dead mother: "Daniel, fear not, my child, God is with you, and who shall be against you? Seek to do good. Be truthful and truth-loving. Yours is a glorious mission."

Mrs. Cook, absolutely convinced that all this was the work of the devil, told Daniel that she could take no more of it. "Leave my house and take your devilish spirits with you!" she said.

He immediately left his aunt's home, going to Willimantic, a town nearby, where he stayed with friends. His reputation as a young medium had spread, and numerous people came to see him.

Up to this point we have to depend solely upon Daniel Home's own account for the strange things that happened to him. Any investigator of the occult—whether a believer or a nonbeliever—must have more support than this. This support began to appear in 1851, when the first newspaper article about Home appeared in a Connecticut paper.

The story reported a séance conducted by Daniel in the home of John Hayden, where the young medium was a guest. The guests were seated around a heavy living-room table with their hands placed on top of it.

At request, the table was moved repeatedly, and in any direction that we asked to have it. All the circle, the Medium [Home] included, had their hands flat upon the table. We looked several times under the table while it was in rapid motion. We saw that no legs or feet had any agency in the movement. . . .

At one time, too, the table was moved *without the Medium's hands or feet touching it at all.*

Daniel immediately learned the disadvantages of publicity. He complained:

> From this time I never had a moment to call my own. In sickness or in health, by day or night, my privacy was intruded on by all comers, some with curiosity, some with higher motives. Men and women of all classes, and all countries; physicians and men of science, ministers of all persuasions, men of literature and of art, all have eagerly sought for proofs . . . of the possibility of spiritual causes acting upon this world of nature.

Home was near the end of his life when he wrote the above statement. He did not exaggerate one bit. Thousands sought him out. Many of these included the most famous men and women of his time.

After leaving his aunt's home, Daniel wandered for the rest of his life. He never made a permanent home anywhere. Forever restless, he seemed to be seeking something he never found. Since he never took money for his séances, he had no means of support. He lived, for the greater part of his life, as the house guest of first one family and then another. He never lacked invitations, for newspapers spread his fame far and near.

In the spring of 1852, Daniel went to Springfield, Massachusetts, to see Henry Gordon, a young medium who was attracting much attention. This is one of only two recorded occasions that Home made contact with another medium. He shunned them most of the time, for he readily acknowledged that most were crooks. Writing of this meeting years later, Daniel said only that he was invited to attend a Gordon séance, but that little happened. This does not seem to be true, as will be detailed later. Home apparently learned a lot from Gordon.

At the Gordon séance, Daniel met Rufus Elmer, a staunch believer in spiritualism. Mrs. Elmer just as strongly disbelieved. Her attitude changed when Daniel went into a trance. He told her the names of all her relatives, of her dead children, and the last words the children spoke before they died. The Elmers were so deeply impressed that they invited Daniel to become their house guest.

While living with the Elmer family, Daniel added to his growing fame. He gave as many as six séances a day. The house was always full of people who came to see him, and those who could not get in crowded around the front door.

During this time a group representing Harvard University asked to attend one of the séances. (A later Harvard investigation condemned spiritualism.) Included in the group was one of the most famous men of the time, William Cullen Bryant. Today Bryant is remembered primarily as a poet—the first American to achieve stature in this field—and he has been called the father of American poetry. He was also a lawyer, but gave that up to become a journalist and editor of the New York *Post*, a position he held for fifty years. He was widely known for his biographies, essays, and prose, in addition to his poetry, which includes the famous "Thanatopsis," "To a Waterfowl," "Death of the Flowers," and others.

The Elmers were awed by the visit of so famous a man. Home did not appear impressed at all. The committee, in addition to Bryant, included B. K. Bliss, William Edwards, and David A. Wells. Home said one was a Harvard professor but did not identify which.

The four men signed a "manifesto" after witnessing the séance. They testified that

1. The table was moved in every possible direction, and with great force, when we could not perceive any cause of motion.

2. The table was forced against each one of us so powerfully as to move us from our positions—together with the chairs we occupied—in all, several feet.

The statement went on to say that Wells and Edwards tried to hold the table still, but could not do so. Then the table "was seen to rise clear of the floor, *and to float in the atmosphere for several seconds.*" Wells, Bliss, and Edwards tried to keep the table down by sitting on it. They were not successful. The floating table was followed by a vibration of the floor, such as might be caused by the rumble of thunder or the firing of cannon.

In conclusion, the committee wrote:

We may observe that Mr. D. D. Home frequently urged us to hold his hands and feet. During these occurrences the room was well lighted. The lamp was frequently placed on or under the table, and every possible opportunity was afforded us for the closest inspection. We admit this one emphatic declaration: *We know that we were not imposed upon nor deceived.*

William Cullen Bryant's was the first signature, indicating that he was the leader of the group. The endorsement of a man like Bryant greatly added to Home's reputation. Simultaneously, his apparent occult powers expanded. Up to that time, he had exhibited second sight, prophecy, and contact with invisible spirits. Now he exhibited spectral lights. This curious phenomenon was attested to by nine men of Springfield, Massachusetts. Their report said, "Lights are produced in a darkened room. Sometimes there appears a gradual illumination, sufficient to disclose very minute objects. At other times, a tremulous phosphorescent light gleams over the walls, and glows emanate from human bodies."

Home claimed that he had often seen these lights, but that this was the first time that they appeared when he was with others.

The second new experience occurred in August 1852, when Home had gone to South Manchester, Connecticut, as the house guest of Ward Cheney.

One of the other guests reported that Home brought them messages from the spirit world by pointing, while in a trance, to letters of the alphabet arranged on a large card. He worked so rapidly that they had difficulty writing down the words as he spelled them out letter by letter. Later the table danced, but this time the movement was so rhythmic that it seemed to be trying to play a tune. The spirit lights danced about the room, and the familiar spirit raps became tremendous noises.

Then came the stunning surprise of the evening. The reporter said: "Suddenly, and without any expectation on the part of the company, Mr. Home was suddenly taken up in the air! I had hold of his hand at the time. I and others felt his feet—they were lifted a foot from the floor! He shook from head to foot, apparently with the contending emotions of joy and fear."

Home was then raised a second time. After he was returned to the floor, he was raised still a third time, and on this occasion he went high enough to touch the ceiling with his hand.

The reporter added to his account: "I omitted to state that these latter demonstrations were made in response to a request of mine that the spirits would give us something that would satisfy everyone in the room of their presence."

The effect upon the assembled guests were enormous. In later years levitation, as it was called, became a very popular stage trick. Actually Jean Eugene Robert-Houdin, using an old Hindu method, had floated his son on a Paris stage about four years before Home levitated himself during this Connecticut séance. Still later John Nevil Maskelyne, the British magician, floated over the head of his audience in London's Egyptian Hall. However, these were stage tricks, performed at a distance from their audiences. Home rose in the air in an unprepared room. His audience stood right beside him, and they were permitted to touch his body. No one ever detected any mechanical contrivance that kept Home suspended. There were, of course, plenty who accused the young medium of trickery, but they were unable to tell how he did it. (See Chapter 14 for a discussion of some suggested methods Home might have employed.)

5

MUSIC
AND A
VISION OF DEATH

Home had been sickly from birth. Time and again his work was interrupted by illness, and he suffered from tuberculosis that was more advanced in one lung than in the other. This may have been the reason he found his "power," as he called it, leaving him for varying periods of time. He was just probably too ill to work at it. He could, of course, also use this "loss of power" as an excuse when he did not want to perform.

This period of his life was characterized by a restlessness that would not permit him to stay in one place very long. He was constantly on the move, making a profession of being a house guest. In later years Sir Arthur Conan Doyle, creator of Sherlock Holmes and an ardent believer in Home, claimed the young medium had a small private income. This was not enough to support him, however.

Despite his difficult financial position, Home continued to refuse offers of money to perform. He would work only as an invited guest on equal footing with his host and other guests. He generally moved in the upper levels of society. However, in one period in New York City, he delighted in going among the poor and bringing joy to bereaved mothers by seeming to bring messages from their dead children.

As time went on, hundreds of mediums who appeared after the Fox sisters' experiences ushered in the age of spiritualism were proved fakes. Many were crooks preying on the credulity of people by appearing to offer financial advice from the grave. This advice often took the form of advising the living to trust their money to the medium, who promptly stole it. Home was also attacked by disbelievers. But in every case his detractors were confounded. He did not convince every doubter, but he did demonstrate that he was definitely different from the usual run of mediums.

Among those who investigated Home was a group called the New York Conference for Spiritualism. Among its members were Dr. John Gray, Dr. Robert Hare of the University of Pennsylvania, and Judge John W. Edmonds of the New York Supreme Court.

The following is said to be an extract from one of the conference's reports:

On the table around which we were seated, were loose papers, a lead pencil, two candles and a glass of water. The table was used by the spirits in responding to our questions. The first peculiarity we observed was that however violently the table was moved everything on it retained its position.

When we had duly observed this, the table, which was mahogany and perfectly smooth, was elevated to an angle of about 30 degrees. It was held there, with everything remaining on it as before. . . . The table was repeatedly made to resume its ordinary position and then again its inclination as before.

> They [the active spirits] were then asked to elevate the table to the same angle as before, and to detach the pencil, retaining everything else upon the table. The table was elevated, the pencil rolled off, and everything else remained.

They continued playing this game, asking for different objects to roll off the table while the others remained. This could easily be duplicated today with a specially wired table and electromagnets embedded in the articles, released one at a time by cutting switches. Electromagnetism was in use for magic tricks at this time. The Frenchman Robert-Houdin used them to make an iron box alternately light and heavy.

These demonstrations made a deep impression on Judge Edmonds. He was so impressed that he later contributed an introduction to the second series of Home's memoirs.

Tables that tipped without spilling their contents were a novel touch. Home continued to add interest to his séances by adding new tricks, such as the levitation demonstrations, and later the stunning demonstration when he apparently floated out a window and back in another window on the third floor of a house in London.

In 1853, while in Boston, Home added still another unusual demonstration. This was spirit music. He claimed it first came to him as he slept, filling the room with harmony so loud it awoke others in the house. He said the spirit music did not awaken him at first. He knew of it only from what others told him they had heard.

This spectral music gradually developed until it was heard at Daniel's séances. Then from unseen music, the manifestations became visible—a guitar that apparently played itself. This happened during a séance for Judge Edmonds' New York Conference. A guitar in the corner of the room was seen to move. Daniel placed it on the table before them.

"In this position," the conference report said, "the guitar was played upon repeatedly." No hands were seen near it. The report continued: "There was no chance for trick. The room was sufficiently lighted for all to see the exact position of every person and thing in the room."

The writer went on to say that the playing was adequate "but not the highest grade of the art." Evidently, the spirit-guitarist—if indeed that's what it was—took some lessons, for later another report of a different séance told of a guitar of "a size and weight somewhat unusual" that played itself:

> The guitar, at a distance of five or six feet from the party, *was played upon exquisitely*, and for several minutes, by some power other than that of anyone bodily present.
> The instrument was partly in shadow and the hand that swept the strings could not be seen; but the *music* was surpassingly beautiful. It was of character entirely new to those who listened, and was sweeter, softer, and more harmonious than anything I have ever heard. Portions of it were filled with a certain soft and wild melody that seemed to be the echo of other music far away, and for the exquisite sweetness of which there are no words.

The author of this report said that in his excitement he leaned forward and accidently extinguished the lamp. (With old-fashioned kerosine lamps, this can occur if something momentarily blocks the top of the glass chimney, thus cutting off the flow of air around the wick. This is probably what happened.) The author said, "But as a good light was reflected upon all of us from a grate of glowing coals directly in front of the party, it was decided not to break the circle to relight the lamp. The séance went on."

The guitar was removed to the opposite corner of the room. This was to see if it could still play at a distance from the medium. This was not done because any of the party suspected Home of trickery. They could see him clearly and he had not been involved, so far as they could tell, in the mysterious playing. A medium was supposed to have certain qualities, not shared by ordinary people, which permitted spirits to contact them. They were curious to know if this effect could be felt across a longer distance. It could, for the guitar played while standing in a corner eleven feet away.

Spiritualism, both in the past and today, has been so riddled with fraud that a serious investigator—whether a believer or a nonbeliever—will approach any manifestation of spirit power with an extremely cautious and skeptical attitude. In the case of Home, we must depend upon accounts written, in some cases, over 125 years ago by people whose powers of observation are unknown to us. Were they fooled? Did they really see what they *thought* they saw? In a time of great excitement—and "contact with spirits" *is* exciting—were they open to suggestion from the medium, thereby seeing things and hearing things that were not there at all?

Later investigators who were not there have thought so. On the other hand, supporters of Home insist that he might have fooled the ignorant, the unwary, and those ardent spiritualists who wanted desperately to believe. But could he have consistently fooled such men as newspaper-editor-poet William Cullen Bryant, a trained lawyer like Judge John Edmonds, and some of the most noted scientists of his day?

When we study these reports today, line by line and word by word, this account of the spirit guitarist is the first indication of possibly trickery. This is in the words of the writer "a guitar, of a size and weight somewhat unusual . . ." Immediately our skeptical minds seize on the idea that there may have been a clockwork mechanism inside that provided the "spirit music." More than 125 years before Home, the British magician Christopher Pinchbeck was performing remarkable clockwork tricks. Jean Eugene Robert-Houdin exhibited some equally remarkable ones. One of these was sold to P. T. Barnum, the famous American circus man, around 1850. Music boxes were also popular through the eighteenth and nineteenth centuries and still can be seen today.

However, in all fairness to Daniel Home, we must say that there is no proof that he had a music box operated by clockwork in his spirit guitar. But we must admit that he has given us ground for suspicion in using an unusual type of instrument for this performance.

Different observers have assured us that the instrument produced music, but none told us definitely that they saw the strings depressed against the frets, or the strings vibrating under the force of an invisible pick.

Up to this point we can offer a possible explanation for the spirit music. What followed next is not so easily explained.

The guitar rose from its position eleven feet away from the circle of observers. It floated across to the circle, dipping to touch Home on the forehead.

"Well, if I did not *see* this myself, I wouldn't believe it on any other testimony!" cried one of the observers.

As if to acknowledge the surprised statement, the guitar moved over and tapped the speaker three times upon the shoulder. The reporter of this séance claimed he then saw an indistinct outline of a hand holding the guitar.

It was evidently *a lady's hand*—very thin, very pale. . . .
The hand afterwards came and *shook hands* with each of
us present. I felt it minutely. It was tolerably well and
symmetrically made, though not perfect; and it was soft
and warm. IT ENDED AT THE WRIST.

In 1853 Daniel Home was twenty years old. He had been before the public as a medium for three years. Still he was restless, unable to stay in any one place for more than a few weeks.

Home was highly regarded by those who took him in as a house guest. All remained his staunch supporters throughout their lives. One aged couple offered to adopt him and make him their heir. He gently but firmly refused. In another case a Swedenborgian minister wanted Home to study for the ministry in his Church. Daniel considered this for a time, but refused after his mother's spirit advised against it. Others offered him various positions. He rejected them all.

In the summer of 1853 Daniel went to live with three friends who were studying at the Theological Institute at Newburgh, New York. He did not take part in any studies, however. He seems to have spent most of his time in meditation. During this period, he had a curious vision. There is no support for this except his own statement as to what happened.

The area around the institute was very beautiful. Daniel liked to go where he could sit and watch the Hudson River flowing down toward the sea. Many times he stayed until after dark, delighting in watching lights go on in the farmhouses below the bluff on which he sat. One evening, while he sat watching the lights in the farmhouse windows, he began to think of death. It was still in his mind when he returned to his quarters. As he lay in bed, he looked out the window and saw a beautiful star twinkling in the sky.

He was then gripped by a strange feeling. "I remember asking myself," he wrote later, "whether I was asleep or no. Then to my amazement I heard a voice." He recognized the voice, but did not identify it. We get the impression that it was his young sister, who had died many years ago. The spirit girl said, "Fear not, Daniel, I am near you. The vision you are about to have is that of death, yet you will not die. Your spirit must again return to your body in a few hours. Trust in God and his good angels. All will be well."

Her voice died away. Daniel felt his soul slipping. He tells us that he tried to cling to existence. He said he was not afraid of death, and that he trusted the guardian angel who had spoken to him. What he feared was the things he might find out "which might disturb my future life."

His body became numb, but his mind increased in activity. His spirit body separated from his earthly body. The body he was quitting appeared to be composed of "thousands of electrical scintillations" that "took the form of currents, darting their rays over the body in a manner most marvelous." The only link between the earth body and the spirit body "seemed to be a silvery-like light, which proceeded from the brain."

The voice that had spoken to him before now said, "Death is but a second birth, corresponding in every respect to the natural birth. Should the uniting link now be severed, you could never again enter the body. As I have told you, however, this is not to be. . . . God is love; and still his children doubt Him. Has He not said,

'Knock, and it shall be opened unto you: seek, and ye shall find?' His words must be taken as they are spoken. . . . Be very calm, for in a few minutes you will see us all, but do not touch us, be guided by one who is appointed to go with you, for I must remain with your body."

A strange light then rose about. "Never did earthly sun shed such rays, strong in beauty, soft in love, warm in life-giving glow. . . . This heavenly light came from those I saw standing about me. Yet the light was not of their creating, but was shed on them from a higher and purer source."

A spirit Home had known on earth conducted him on an aerial tour. The purpose seems to have been to acquaint him with how the spirit world watches over their loved ones on earth. They floated on a purple cloud until Home could see a rustic cabin below. The walls were transparent to him. The people who lived there were asleep.

"I saw various spirits who were watching over these sleepers. One spirit was endeavoring to impress his son where to find a lost relic. In an adjoining room I saw one who was tormented by dreams, but they were but the product of a diseased body."

Home was then taken back to his own body. He protested at leaving the spirit world so soon. He was told that time passes more slowly in the afterlife and that he had been with them for eleven hours. They returned his spirit to his body with this admonition: "Return to earth, love your fellow-creatures, love truth, and in so doing, you will serve the God of infinite love, who careth for and loveth all."

He came to his earthly consciousness and saw that the star he had been watching before his spectral adventure "had now changed to the sun, four hours above the horizon."

Naturally, such a story as this aroused great controversy. It brought denunciations of everything from an outright lie to hallucinations caused by a sick mind—and Home *was* ill at the time. By his own admission, he had been thinking hard about death before this adventure.

In reply to his critics, he said merely, "I give these facts as they occurred. Let others comment on them as they may. I have only to add, that nothing could ever convince me that this was an illusion or a delusion. The remembrance of those hours is as fresh in my mind now, as at the moment they took place."

Home's health continued to give him trouble. At one time he considered starting medical studies, but his left lung was giving him such trouble that he was advised against it. Instead, he turned to a new adventure that would finally bring him the peace of mind he sought by fulfilling an ambition that had long been in his heart.

The event that set it in motion was the arrival in the United States of the distinguished British editor and author William Makepeace Thackeray, best remembered today for the novel *Vanity Fair*. Thackeray was on a lecture tour. While he was in New York, friends took him to see Home. The Englishman was entranced. He sent an enthusiastic letter to friends in England. Although spiritualism had been a popular rage in the United States for five years, it had not caught on yet in England.

This was surprising, for ghosts and haunted houses were very much a part of British culture. It was just that English ghosts were frightening things, whereas Home's spirits were friendly.

The meeting with Thackeray turned Home's thoughts toward England. It must be admitted that there was considerable snobbery in the young man's makeup. He never forgot that he had a connection—left-handed though it was—with Scottish nobility through his Hume ancestry. He had an intense hunger to walk with nobles and kings, something most unlikely for one living in the United States. This may account for his inability to put down roots. In any event, it now became his burning ambition to visit England and the European continent.

In January 1855 his cough increased, indicating a worsening of his lung trouble. He said that his doctors recommended a trip to England for his health. This seems peculiar advice. London, with its thick fogs saturated with poisonous coal smoke, was the poorest possible place for anyone with lung trouble. But he was determined to go, and a family he was staying with paid his fare. He sailed on March 31, 1855, in the ship *Africa*.

He was twenty-two years old, and headed for international fame that would be accompanied by the bitterest denunciations from some very famous people.

6

BRITISH FRIENDS, BRITISH ENEMIES

Daniel was still ill when the ship docked in England on April 9, 1855. He was in very low spirits. He tells how he felt:

> I stood there alone, with not one friend to welcome me. I was broken down in health. My hopes and fairest dreams of youth, all, as I thought, forever fled. The only prospect I had was that of a few month's suffering, and then to pass from the earth. I had this strange power, also, which made a few look with pity on me as a poor deluded being. Others were not chary in treating me as a base imposter.

Home goes on to tell us that he went back to his cabin and sought relief in prayer. Then, feeling better, he left the ship and in the evening arrived at Cox's Hotel in Jermyn Street, London. William Cox, the proprietor, was deeply interested in spiritualism. Friends in the United States had written glowing introductions for Home, and Thackeray had spoken enthusiastically to

Cox about Home. The hotelier welcomed Daniel effusively and put him up rent free—a necessity, since Home arrived in England without a cent.

The arrangement was really a good business deal for Cox. Crowds flocked to the hotel to see the amazing young man from the States. The interest was gratifying, but Home had come to Europe to meet the nobility. This opportunity came three weeks after his arrival, when Lord Henry Brougham sent word to Cox that he would like to meet Home. The note said that Brougham would like to bring a friend, Sir David Brewster, a noted scientist of the day.

Home was delighted. Lord Brougham was an important politician and former Lord Chancellor of England. The brougham carriage, a four-wheeled affair in which the driver sits outside the closed compartment, was named after him. Henry Brougham was then seventy-seven years old—not ninety, as some Home biographers have claimed, for he was born in 1778.

Unfortunately, Daniel Home did not know much about Sir David Brewster. He was a strongly opinionated man, eager in all cases to build his own scientific reputation at the expense of others. Had Daniel known the bitterness and trouble that Brewster would cause him, he might have refused to meet the pair, despite his hunger to associate with titles. However, he was not aware of Sir David's character. He did assume, because Brewster was a scientist, that Lord Brougham was bringing Brewster along to test Home. This did not trouble Daniel at all. He had full confidence that he could pass any test, just as he had done with the New York Conference and the Harvard group, who had been assisted by the famous William Cullen Bryant.

Brougham and Brewster came in the afternoon. Daniel

invited Mr. Cox, the innkeeper, to join them. They sat down at a card table. Home invited his guests to inspect the table, look under it for hidden machinery, or to make any other tests and inspection that they wished. Both Brougham and Brewster declined to do so.

The séance began, but it was far from the usual dramatic event that one had grown to expect from Home. There was first an exhibition of spirit rapping and answering of questions by raps. After a half hour of this, Home was seized by a severe coughing spell. He excused himself and went upstairs to get a handkerchief.

When he returned, Brewster suggested that they change to a larger, heavier table. Daniel was amused, for he knew that Brewster suspected that the card table had been rigged in advance. He readily agreed and again suggested that his visitors inspect the table. Again they declined. The visitors sat down and placed their fingers on the table as before. Instead of the previous raps, the table began to dance up and down. Then an accordion sailed across the room, playing a tune as it came. Brougham looked astonished. Brewster, although in better control of his reactions than Brougham, stared in surprise.

At the conclusion of the séance, Brewster said to Cox (so Cox claimed), "Sir, this upsets the philosophy I've held for fifty years." Lord Brougham expressed his astonishment, but made no other comment. Home was delighted. Lord Brougham was the most distinguished man for whom he had given a séance. He secretly hoped that this would aid his entrée into royal circles. He did not dare to hope that Queen Victoria would give him an audience, but he did hope to meet lesser members of the royal family.

About a month after this séance, Daniel met Sir John Snaith Rymer, a prominent lawyer. He invited Home to become his house guest. Rymer lived with his family in Ealing, a London suburb. Home quickly became like one of the family, playing with the Rymer children and calling Mrs. Rymer Mother and Mr. Rymer Papa.

Brougham and Brewster attended a séance at the Rymers. Other guests included Fanny (Frances) Trollope and her son, Thomas A. Trollope. Mrs. Trollope was a popular writer of the day and the mother of Anthony Trollope, author of *Barchester Towers* and other famous books. Mrs. Trollope was particularly noted for her dislike of Americans. Soon after publication of her travel book, *Domestic Manners of the Americans*, the press in the United States referred to Fanny as "old Lady Vinegar."

Mrs. Trollope's son, Thomas Augustus, was a large man. His beard was so luxuriant that it was said that neither he nor anyone else knew what he really looked like under its camouflage. Trollope had a very bombastic manner and an opinion on every subject, and he delivered that opinion with considerable force.

Mrs. Trollope, true to the critical spirit of her book, disliked Home because he came from America. This was in contrast to most women Daniel met. They usually wanted to mother him.

Trollope, on the other hand, found Home intensely interesting. It was he who had brought his mother all the way from Florence, Italy, to meet the medium. Home had been the subject of lively discussions among the British expatriates who made up the Florence literary colony.

In his memoirs, *What I Remember*, published in 1887, Trollope described Daniel as "a young American, rather tall, with a loosely put together figure, red hair, large and clear but not bright blue eyes." He added that Home had a sensual mouth, lanky cheeks, and the complexion of a person with medical disorders. Trollope also found Home courteous and always willing to talk about his spiritualistic gifts. However, Home was "unable or unwilling to formulate or enter into discussion on any theory respecting them."

Home also stopped discussing his "vision of death." He continued to tell it, but took the position, "This is what happened. *You* explain it." He did not, out of politeness, put it so bluntly, but this is what his manner implied.

Later, during a bitter battle of newspaper letters, both Home and Brewster gave their version of what happened at the séance. Since their versions differ considerably, it is perhaps better to examine what happened through the eyes of Thomas Trollope, since he was in a position to be less biased.

Trollope said that the party had supper and that Daniel seemed more inclined to flirt with one of the young girls present than to pay much attention to the others. Trollope got the impression that Home was a "petted inmate of the household."

After they had dined, the party moved to the drawing room. They took their places around a very heavy mahogany table in the familiar manner of spiritualist séances. Following the usual spirit raps, the table began to move. Of this Trollope said, "Although an ordinary man could have raised either end of the table, I am persuaded that no man could have raised it bodily, unless perhaps by placing his shoulders under the center of it."

Trollope does not record any other spirit manifestation, although others did. In any event, the evening appeared on the surface to have been another success. The guests were impressed. Both Brougham and Sir David Brewster shook hands with Home and thanked him for the evening. Brewster made no comment. The other guests left talking about the levitation of the table, a handkerchief that had five knots tied in it (presumably by spirits), and an accordion that played itself.

This séance took place in July. In October it became the focal point for a bitter battle fought in the pages of various newspaper letter columns. Home credits the vindictiveness of Brewster for this fight, but it is clear that Home himself brought it about. He sent an account of the British séances to an American spiritualist magazine. We do not know if Home exaggerated his accomplishments in England or if the editor embellished the account. In any event, the article implied that both Lord Brougham and Sir David Brewster had completely endorsed Home's accomplishment.

Unfortunately, this account was picked up and reprinted in the English *Morning Advertiser*. Home admitted in his autobiography that this was "a somewhat inaccurate account of what had occurred."

On September 29, 1855, Sir David immediately wrote a letter to the editor of the *Advertiser*. The letter appeared with the following editor's note as a preface:

We publish the following letter from Sir David Brewster, relative to the article which we lately quoted from an American paper, in which Lord Brougham and Sir David were represented as believing in spirit manifestations. This alleged belief was illustrated by certain things which were said of the two distinguished individuals in connexion with a display of "spiritual agency in July last, at Ealing.

The editor's note went on to say that the paper sent a copy of the clipping from *The New York Spiritualist* to Lord Brougham for his comment. They received a courteous letter from his lordship "in which he repudiates the idea of his being a believer, *in the sense ascribed to him.*"

Part of Brewster's irritated note to the *Advertiser* read:

> It is also true that I saw at Cox's Hotel, in company with Lord Brougham, and at Ealing, in company with Mrs. Trollope, several mechanical effects which I was unable to explain. But though I could not account for these effects, I never thought of ascribing them to spirits stalking beneath the drapery of the table; and I saw enough to satisfy myself that they could all be produced by human hands and feet, and to prove to others that some of them, at least, had such an origin.
>
> Were Mr. Home to assume the character of the Wizard of the West, I would enjoy his exhibition as much as that of other conjurors. [The allusion to Wizard of the West was to compare Home with the famous John Anderson, who billed himself as the Wizard of the North. Anderson was an internationally famous conjuror and stage magician.] But when he pretends to possess the power of introducing among the feet of his audience the spirits of the dead, of bringing them into physical communication with their dearest relatives, and of revealing the secrets of the grave, he insults religion and common sense, and tampers with the most sacred feelings of his victims.

When this letter appeared in the *Advertiser*, Home was in Italy as the house guest of the Trollopes. Fanny Trollope's first unfavorable opinion of Home had given way to admiration, at least for a time.

In London Daniel's friends rushed to his defense. William Cox wrote the editor an open letter to Sir David:

. . .I have a distinct recollection of the astonishment which both Lord Brougham and yourself expressed, and your remarkable and emphatic exclamation to me:— *"Sir, this upsets the philosophy of fifty years."* . . .

If the subject be beyond your powers of reasonable explanation, leave it to others; for it is not just or generous to raise the cry of imposture in a matter you cannot explain, taking advantage of your character to place humbler men in a false position, by allowing the world to think they were, by ignorance or design, parties to so gross and impudent a fraud.

Brewster struck back with an angry denial: "I may once for all admit that both Lord Brougham and myself freely acknowledge that *we were puzzled with Mr. Home's performances,* and could not account for them. . . . If we had been permitted to take a peep under the drapery of Mr. Cox's table, we should have been spared the mortification of this confession." (This statement is unkind of Sir David, for all agree that Home invited both men to look under the table. Later evidence shows that Brewster did look under the table during the Ealing séance.)

Brewster then denied that the spirit accordion had floated to Lord Brougham—it was placed in his lordship's hand. He denied that the accordion played a tune. "It merely squeaked," he wrote. He denied that he said, "This upsets the philosophy of fifty years." He said that these were the words used by another man "and very untruly put in my mouth by Mr. Cox."

In giving his version of the séance, Brewster wrote:

When all our hands were upon the table noises were heard, rapping in abundance. Finally when we rose up the table actually rose, as appeared to me, from the ground. The result I do not pretend to explain. But rather than believe that spirits made the noise, I will conjecture that the raps were produced by Mr. Home's toes, which, as will be seen, were active on another occasion. And rather than believe that spirits raised the table, I will conjecture that it was done by the agency of Mr. Home's feet, which were always below it.

Brewster claimed the spirit accordion would only play when Home held it under the table. He cited a bell supposedly rung by spirits. It was placed on the floor at Brewster's feet. He said:

> I placed my feet around it to form an angle, to catch an intrusive apparatus. The bell did not ring; but when taken to a place near Mr. Home's feet, it speedily came across, and placed its handle in my hand. This was amusing.
>
> It did the same thing, bunglingly, to Lord Brougham, but knocking itself against his lordship's knuckles, and after a jingle, it fell. How these effects were produced neither Lord Brougham nor I could say, but I conjecture that they may be produced by machinery attached to the lower extremities of Mr. Home.

He mentioned the time Home left the table, claiming the medium had gone upstairs to hide new apparatus in his clothing. (Home, it will be remembered, claimed he had gone for a handkerchief because he was coughing.) Brewster then took up the handkerchief that had knotted itself at the Ealing performance.

The handkerchief had early been collected from one of those present. Home asked the spirits to tie knots in it as a sign of their presence. He had earlier done this before leaving America. At that time the handkerchief had vanished and reappeared tied in the form of a crude rag doll. One of the women present cried that it was the kind of thing her dead daughter had been fond of making.

In the Ealing case Brewster said they had all forgotten the handkerchief because of the other things that were happening. Then a half hour later, the handkerchief suddenly dropped to the center of the table. Five knots had been tied in it. One of Home's hands had been holding the accordion. The other was in plain view on top of the table.

"How were those knots tied, unless by spirits?" Brewster asked and then attempted to answer his own question.

> Mr. Home continued to hold the accordion, as we thought, but he might have placed it on the floor, and had his right hand free under the table for any purpose. . . . During the half hour's absence of the handkerchief, Mr. Home, three or four times, gave a start and looked wildly at the company, saying, "Dear me, how the spirits are troubling me." At the same time, he put down his left hand as if to push away his tormentors, or soothe the limb around which they had been clustering. He had, therefore, both his hands beneath the table for a sufficient time to tie the five marvellous knots.
>
> I offer these facts for the spiritual instruction of yourself, Mr. Cox, and for the information of the public.

The argument continued with additional charges and countercharges on both sides. Lord Brougham refused to enter into it at all, except for his initial statement denying he was correctly quoted on his belief in spiritualism. Solicitor Rymer, being a lawyer, sought additional witnesses. He wrote Trollope in Italy, asking a statement from him.

Trollope replied in a letter from Florence, dated October 23, 1855, that it was painful to come from his tranquil obscurity into "the noise and wholly inconclusive bickerings of paper warfare." However, he found it impossible to refuse his testimony to facts he had witnessed.

He pleaded no knowledge to what had happened at the Cox's Hotel séance, but at the Rymer home in Ealing he had seen a very heavy dining table move about "in a most extraordinary manner."

"Sir David was urged, both by Mr. Home and by yourself, to look under the table, and while he was so looking, the table was much moved. While he [Sir David Brewster] was looking, and while the table was moving, Brewster avowed that he saw the movement."

After taking up other points raised by Brewster, Trollope said:

> I should not, my dear Sir, do all that duty requires of me in this case were I to conclude without stating very solemnly that after very many opportunities of witnessing and investigating the phenomena caused by, or happening to Mr. Home, I am wholly convinced that be what may their origins, and cause, and nature, they are not caused by any fraud, machinery, juggling, illusion, or trickery, on his part.

The newspaper war slowly petered out, but the feud between Daniel Home and Sir David Brewster continued to simmer under the surface. Just as it was Home who had started it before with his story in the American spiritualist magazine, he stirred the pot again in 1862, when he published his autobiography, *Incidents in My Life*. He included an appendix titled *"Sir David Brewster."* In it Home collected all the evidence for himself and attempted to refute Brewster's arguments point by point.

This might have passed without another explosion, for Home was only rehashing all the material that had appeared in the *Advertiser* seven years before. However, Home chose to attack Sir David's honesty and professional reputation as a scientist. He accused Brewster of trying to steal credit for invention of the stereoscope (a method of viewing photographs in three dimension) from Sir Charles Wheatstone. Sir Charles is also the inventer of the concertina, the harmonica, and the Wheatstone bridge, a device for measuring resistances in electrical circuits.

He next accused Brewster of trying to grab credit for the use of the Fresnel lens in developing the modern lighthouse, an honor belonging to the noted lighthouse engineer, Robert Stevenson, grandfather of Robert Louis Stevenson, author of *Treasure Island* and other works.

At this time Home was in France and outside the jurisdiction of British civil courts. Brewster turned to Home's publishers, Longman and Company, sending this letter:

> My attention has been called to a malignant libel upon my character, published by you in a Book entitled *Incidents of My Life* [Sic]. By D. D. Home. . . . As the resident head of Edinburgh University, I need not point out to you the effect of such a libel upon my feelings and usefulness. . . . You must have been aware, that in publishing this libel, you inflicted on me a very grave injury.
>
> As Mr. Home is not in England, I am under the necessity of taking such steps against you as my friends may think necessary.

As it happened, Sir David never got around to prosecuting his case. In any event, the character of Brewster was such that public sympathy was with Home.

Equally bitter was another feud that grew from the

Ealing séances. This one was with the famous poet
Robert Browning, and also eventually erupted in print.

There was another disappointment in the Ealing
séances, although it did not become a public scandal.
This was Daniel's failure to impress Sir Edward
Bulwer-Lytton. Daniel was disappointed because
Bulwer-Lytton had been a lifelong student of the occult,
and it would have been a triumph to have him on one's
side. Home's meeting with Bulwer-Lytton came before
his fight with Robert Browning.

7

A CURIOUS WRITER
AND AN ANGRY POET

Edward George Earle Bulwer-Lytton was born in 1803. He was the son of General Bulwer, who had little use for him. His mother was a daughter of the wealthy Lytton family. The Lyttons likewise had little use for the boy. As a result, Edward grew up lonely, taking his greatest delight in books. He grew up, studied at Cambridge, and set out to be a traveler and poet.

During these years, young Bulwer-Lytton came into contact with occult societies and was said to have dabbled a bit in black magic and sorcery—a not unpopular pursuit for young men of his time. While still in his teens, he had met a girl in Ealing, seeing her secretly beside a stream removed from the sight of other people. One day she did not come back to their meeting place. Much later, he received a letter from her. She had been forced into an unhappy marriage and was dying. She professed her undying love for Bulwer-Lytton and asked that he visit her grave.

Sir Edward Bulwer-Lytton, author of *The Last Days of Pompeii*, was interested in Home, but never quite believed in spiritualism despite many years' study of mystic and occult subjects.

He did search out her grave, spending the entire night beside it. Strange things were supposed to have happened that night, but he never gave any details. Because of his known interest in the occult, we can suppose that he met, or thought he met, his lost love.

Later in Europe he joined a gypsy band to be near a girl who had told his fortune. For a while it appeared that he might marry and stay with her. However, the gypsy men disliked having an outsider among them and drove him away. He left, carrying with him his gypsy sweetheart's prophecy: "You will never want and will be much before the world, but you will never receive the honors that are your due. You will hunger for love all your life, but it will only bring you sorrow."

And it happened as she predicted. He lost the three loves who might have made him happy—the girl who died, the gypsy, and a French girl. Then he married, when he was twenty-four, an English woman ill suited for a man of his type. He began writing novels and became a Member of Parliament. At one time a pamphlet he wrote was credited with winning the election for his Liberal party. This brought him the offer of a government position. He turned it down to concentrate on his writing, although from time to time he returned to Parliament.

In 1833, broken in health, he went to Italy to recuperate. While there he visited Pompeii. The fabulous ruins, only lately recovered from the volcanic ash that had buried it in Roman times, seemed to talk to him. He returned to England and wrote the novel for which he is best remembered today, *The Last Days of Pompeii.*

Finally in 1842 he published *Zanoni,* in which he put all he had learned of the occult. Zanoni, the hero of the novel, was a superman. He had acquired an elixir that prolonged his life and kept him looking ever young. However, to accomplish this he had to condition his body properly by renouncing all affection, desires, and earthly love. The elixir also gave him the ability to foresee any danger to himself, which he needed, for the elixir only prolonged youth and body. It did not make him immortal from accidental or manmade death.

Zanoni lived for several centuries, until he fell in love with a beautiful girl. When she is threatened in the French Reign of Terror, he happily sacrifices his life for her.

A brief outline cannot do justice to the book's weird atmosphere and occult strains. Although rambling and difficult, it is still read for its Rosicrucian mysticism. It was said that Bulwer-Lytton put much of himself into the character of Zanoni, and the book was his favorite of everything he wrote.

Daniel Home had read *Zanoni*. He had been fascinated by the character of the ageless man who used occult powers for good. He felt a kinship to the character and through him with the author. For this reason he wanted very much to impress Bulwer-Lytton. The writer was then a man of fifty-two years, and had recently resumed his political career. He had joined the Conservative party in 1851 and had been elected MP from Hereford in 1852. There was talk that he was in line for an important post in the government.

Bulwer-Lytton was also interested in Home. Part of this was due to the writer's lifelong interest in the occult. In addition, Bulwer-Lytton was seeking a character for a new book that would be a return to the mysticism of *Zanoni*, and he thought he might find it in the person of the young Scots-American medium. The book was finally published six years later, in 1861, under the title *A Strange Story*. He did not use Home's character, but some of the séance scenes read like a description of Home's work.

Sir Edward—he did not become Lord Lytton until 1866—came with his son to the Rymer house in Ealing to view a Home séance. Bulwer-Lytton was guarded in his comments about what he saw, probably because of his political position at the time. According to the account left by Home, the spirit manifestations of the evening centered almost entirely around the famous visitor.

The rapping on the table was stronger than usual. The alphabet board was brought out so Home could point out the letters as they were communicated to him by the spirit. Bulwer-Lytton was permitted to question the spirit.

"What spirit is present?" the author asked.

"I am the spirit who influenced you to write *Zanoni!*" was the reply.

If Home had been faking this answer, he would have been taking a big chance of exposure, for there had been nothing said about how anyone or anything had influenced the writing of the famous occult novel. All Bulwer-Lytton had said was that the idea came to him in a dream. However, it was common knowledge that Bulwer-Lytton had drawn much material from his personal association with Rosicrucianism.

All the novelist said, in reply to the surprising assertion that he had been helped by the spirit, was "Indeed." Then Bulwer-Lytton added, "I wish you would give some tangible proof of your presence."

"Will you take my hand?" Home spelled out the spirit's message by pointing to the alphabet letters in rapid succession. He—through long practice—could do this so fast that the person detailed to write down the message had difficulty keeping up with him.

"Oh, yes, of course," Bulwer-Lytton said quickly.

Home's spirits operated under the table. The famous author put his hand under the table. It was immediately seized in a strong grip. Bulwer-Lytton leaped to his feet in startled surprise. Home wrote later:

> He exhibited a momentary suspicion that a trick had been played upon him. Seeing, however, that all the persons around him were sitting with their hands quietly reposing on the table, he recovered his composure. Offering an apology for the uncontrollable excitement caused by such an unexpected demonstration, he resumed his seat.

The spirit then spoke again through Home's alphabet reading.

The message said, "We wish you to believe in—"

When the words stopped here, Bulwer-Lytton asked, "In what am I to believe? In the medium?"

The answer was no, and Bulwer-Lytton asked, "In the manifestations?" Again the answer was no. At this point the writer felt a gentle tap on his knee. Putting his hand down quickly, he found his answer in a small cross lying on his knee. It was made of cardboard. When the séance started, it had been lying on a small table at the opposite side of the room.

Bulwer-Lytton looked at the crude cross thoughtfully. He turned to Mrs. Rymer and asked his hostess if he might keep the cross as a souvenir of the evening.

"Of course," she replied. She added that it had been made by her young son, who had recently died. She had kept it as a remembrance of his religious devotion.

Home continued his association with Bulwer-Lytton for the next ten years, but was never able to break down the famous writer's reserve. On two occasions he was guest at Bulwer-Lytton's estate. Unlike the others who were so astounded by Home's performances, Bulwer-Lytton had had considerable experience with mediums, sorcerers, and black magicians. He had seen much fraud and fakery—and admittedly much that could not be explained. Thus he found nothing in Home that was really new to him.

Later, when Home introduced his levitation performances, Bulwer-Lytton told his son that this, too, was nothing new. Numerous magical adepts of the past had had the same power. In fact, floating around the stage had become a popular conjuror's trick.

After Home's death, his widow said that Daniel's failure to impress Bulwer-Lytton was a major disappointment of his life. In a book called *Life and Mission of Home,* Mrs. Home said, "Lord Lytton, then Sir E. B. Lytton, was perfectly convinced of the genuineness of the phenomena he witnessed in Mr. Home's presence, and even of their spiritual origin, but was too timid to avow his convictions publicly."

In another book, *The Gift of D. D. Home,* his wife wrote, "Lord Lytton saw the facts of spiritualism through a haze of fancies concerning sylphs, gnomes, 'Dwellers on the Thresholds,' and fiendish or angelic creatures compounded of fire or air."

Bulwer-Lytton kept most of his true thoughts about Home to himself. Not so another famous writer. The English poet Robert Browning also came to an Ealing séance. He left an even more violent enemy of the young medium than Sir David Brewster. Brewster had contented himself with angry letters and a threat of a libel suit. Browning threatened to kill Home on one occasion, and on another claimed he would kick Home like a dog if ever they met again.

On the other hand, Browning's wife, Elizabeth Barrett Browning, believed in Home as ardently as her volatile husband disbelieved.

The romance of Robert Browning and Elizabeth Moulton-Barrett is one of the great love stories of English history. Their remarkable love letters have been preserved—except for the single one in which Browning first spoke of his love for invalid Elizabeth—and published. In addition to the thousands who thrilled to the unfolding love portrayed in the letters, millions more became familiar with this classic romance through the play and motion picture, *The Barretts of Wimpole Street*.

Edward Moulton-Barrett, who lived at 50 Wimpole Street in London, was an absolute family tyrant. Yet despite this, he loved his eldest daughter dearly. This girl, Elizabeth, suffered an accident to her spine when she was twelve, and later the drowning of a beloved brother affected her physically. She became an invalid, rarely leaving her room, where her constant companion was her dog Flush.

She turned to poetry, and in 1840 her father had a collection of her poems privately printed. They were successful, and she became quite famous. In time the poems came to the attention of Robert Browning, then quite some years away from his own fame as a poet. Browning was captivated and asked permission to call upon the poetess to express his appreciation of her art.

He found Elizabeth Moulton-Barrett to be a very tiny thing, with large eyes set in a pale-ivory face framed by long dark hair. A friend said of her that she was "all eyes and hair." Browning fell in love with her, although she was some years older than he.

Browning could not continue to call upon Elizabeth, because her father absolutely would not permit it. Their friendship blossomed into love mostly through letters. They met secretly once a week, when Edward Moulton-Barrett was away. Eventually Browning persuaded her to elope with him to Italy. Her father never forgave her. The letters she wrote him were returned unopened.

During the courtship, Elizabeth poured out her feeling for her lover in a series of forty-two sonnets, which were later known as *Sonnets from the Portuguese*. They were not translations, as their title implies. The title appears to come from a pet name Browning gave her because of Elizabeth's dark hair. He called her his "little Portuguese." She kept the sonnets secret and did not show them to Browning until some time after their marriage.

Sickly as she was, Elizabeth Barrett Browning lived under the constant threat of death, and thought much about life after death. Consequently, Mrs. Browning was greatly interested to hear that a young man from America was apparently proving that death was but the rebirth of the human spirit into another and happier world.

The Brownings first heard of Home while they were still in Italy. They returned to London for a short stay in 1855, and, under Elizabeth's urging, attended a séance at the Rymer home in Ealing. Although still delicate, Mrs. Browning's health had improved considerably after her marriage—indicating, perhaps, that some of her trouble was caused by her mental attitude.

The meeting with the Brownings turned out to be so painful to Home that he made no mention of it at all in his autobiography, *Incidents in My Life*, published in 1863. After this was published, Browning presented a vicious picture of Home in a long poem called, "Mr. Sludge, the Medium." Home replied in his second book of memoirs, *Incidents in My Life, 2nd Series*," published in 1872. In this book Home repeated his previous claims that Browning's enmity was caused by jealousy.

Home wrote:

> Previously to the arrival of the Brownings some of the children had been gathering flowers in the garden, and Miss Rymer and I had made a wreath of clematis. The wreath was lying on the table, at a little distance from that at which we were sitting. The wreath was afterwards put on the table at which we were grouped, but whether naturally or by spirit hands I do not remember.
>
> During the séance this wreath was raised from the table by supernatural power in the presence of us all. Whilst we were watching it, Mr. Browning, who was seated at the opposite end of the table, left his place and came and stood behind his wife.

The wreath moved slowly through the air as the entire group around the table watched breathlessly. It settled on Elizabeth Barrett Browning's head, crowning her with flowers. Browning stood directly behind her as this happened, staring silently at the moving flowers.

Home said:

> Browning expressed no disbelief; as indeed, it was impossible for any one to have any of what was passing under his eyes. Mrs. Browning was much moved, and she, not only then but ever since, expressed her entire belief and pleasure in what then occurred.
>
> It was the remark of all the Rymer family, that Mr.

Browning seemed much disappointed that the wreath was not put upon his own head instead of his wife's, and that his placing himself in the way of where it was being carried, was for the purpose of giving it an opportunity of being placed upon his own brow.

Mrs. Browning gave her own version of what happened in a letter to her sister, Henrietta. Elizabeth cautioned her sister not to mention Home if she wrote back "because it is a tabooed subject in this house—Robert and I taking completely different views, and he being a great deal irritated by any discussion of it."

Elizabeth said that there was not as much activity at the séance she attended as had been reported to her by Bulwer-Lytton's son, a friend of the Brownings. There were some spirit rappings, some mysterious music, a moving table, and the spirit hands that held the soon-to-be-famous wreath of clematis.

Describing the hands holding the flowers, Mrs. Browning said they were large, white as snow, and very beautiful. Mrs. Browning was nearsighted and carried a "looking glass" suspended from a ribbon, which she raised when she wanted to see distant objects more clearly. She wrote to Henrietta, "The hands which appeared at a distance from me I put up my glass to look at—proving it was not a mere mental impression."

She said that she did not touch the hands as they came near her, but at an earlier séance Robert Lytton had done so. The hands were soft, warm and human. (At a different séance another observer claimed he took one of these spirit hands in his. He tried to hold it, but it melted away under his grip and vanished.)

Browning's annoyance was plain, although he said little that night. Then a few days later Home accompanied Mrs. Rymer, who was making some farewell calls before the family left for a seashore vacation. When they came to the Brownings' place, Robert Browning let his temper fly at Home. In the beginning Browning ignored Home's outstretched hand, refusing to shake it.

Mrs. Browning was visibly disturbed by her husband's actions. She took Home's hand in hers, saying, "I am so sorry, but do not blame me!"

Browning, still ignoring Home, said to Mrs. Rymer, "I was singularly dissatisfied with everything I saw at your house the other night!"

"Then why did you not say so at the time?" Home asked.

Browning turned pale with rage, looking—Home said—like a maniac. Home then turned and left the house.

Browning had a somewhat different account of the meeting. He claimed he told Home to get out of his house "or I'll fling you down the stairs!"

Later he told Elizabeth that he would "shoot the scoundrel" if he met Home again. He was still raging at the sound of Home's name three years later when Nathaniel Hawthorne, author of *The Scarlet Letter* and *The House of the Seven Gables*, visited the Brownings in Italy.

Everywhere Hawthorne went in Florence he heard about Home. Many of these people supported the medium, and Elizabeth Barrett Browning was especially eloquent. However, Hawthorne wrote that Browning's arguments against the medium were very logical. But in the end he confessed himself bored by Browning's continual ravings and rantings against Home.

Both to Hawthorne and to others Browning insisted that he had caught Home cheating. Browning's biographer, Betty Miller, said of this claim, "There is no evidence, by the way, that the poet did anything of the kind." This did not keep Browning from continuing to claim that Home produced his "miracles" through an adroit use of his feet.

In 1851 Elizabeth wrote her sister that Browning was working on a long poem, which she had not seen. She was destined never to see it, for Browning kept it hidden until after her death. The poem is overly long, rambling, and difficult to read, but can be found in the complete collection of Browning's poems, if anyone is interested. Arthur Conan Doyle, an admirer of Home, called the poem "doggerel." Entitled "Mr. Sludge, the Medium," it tells of the pitiful pleadings of a medium who has been exposed as a cheat. The opening lines read:

Now don't, sir! Don't expose me! Just this once!
This was the first and only time, I swear,—
Look at me,—see, I kneel—the only time,
I swear I ever cheated,—yes, by the soul!
Of Her who hears (your sainted mother, sir!)
All, except this last accident, was truth.

You've heard what I confess; I don't unsay
A single word: I cheated when I could,
Rapped with my toe-joints, see sham hands at work,
Wrote down names weak in sympathetic ink,
Rubbed odic lights with ends of phosphor-match.
And all the rest.

The entire poem consumes two thousand lines, all condemning a medium called "Mr. Sludge." Although Home's name was not used in the poem, after its publication in 1864 everyone who read it knew that Browning was accusing the now-famous Daniel Dunglas Home. Mrs. Home, in *Life and Mission of Home*, wrote:

Perhaps none of the thousand falsehoods circulated concerning Mr. Home has been more persistently repeated than the assertion that he was found cheating by Mr. Robert Browning. Mr. Browning himself, in his unpoetic effusion, "Mr. Sludge, the Medium," appeared to lend a certain color to the fable. Otherwise, it would have probably died the natural death of slanders that have not a grain of fact in their composition.

Mrs. William Burnet Kinney, wife of an American ambassador, had been greatly impressed by Home. This happened although she came to his séance a confirmed skeptic. She wrote to Browning, asking his opinion of Home. He replied at length, again rehashing the Ealing séance and condemning Home as a fraud. In 1871 Mrs. Kinney wrote Browning to ask his permission to publish his letter.

Browning refused, saying that it would give "that unmitigated scoundrel"—meaning Home—an opportunity to retaliate, with "a fresh vomit of lies." He added that if he ever met Home again, he would probably "soil my shoe by kicking him."

Browning was wrong in claiming, as he often did, that he had caught Home cheating. All authorities agree that he did not. It is possible that his blind rage caused him to convince himself that he had.

On the other hand, Home was equally wrong in claiming that Browning's enmity was caused by jealousy in not being crowned as "The Poet" by the spirit with the garland of flowers. At no time did Browning ever show any jealousy of his wife's poetic fame. In her lifetime she was far more popular as a writer than he was. He took pride in this. It was his own love of Elizabeth Barrett's poetry that had brought them together in the first place.

It is more logical to assume that Browning's rage was caused by Browning's jealousy of his beloved wife's interest in Home.

Other giants of nineteenth-century English literature took varying positions regarding Home. William Makepeace Thackeray supported Home. Alfred Lord Tennyson heard a lot about Home from his brother Frederick Tennyson, a strong believer in spiritualism. Mrs. Home quotes a letter that Home received from an unidentified "well known English medical man" (probably Dr. Garth Wilkinson, an ardent supporter of Home), who wrote:

> I went to lunch with Alfred Tennyson, and had two or three hours' talk with him. . . . He said that if he and you and I could have a sitting or two in daylight, or in a strong artificial light, and he convinced himself of the *facts*, he should have no hesitation in proclaiming his belief in any way. Meantime he says that he is much more inclined to believe than to disbelieve. He had all those tales from Browning, including one that you went on your knees, wept, and confessed your imposture in a certain thing. I told him Browning was mad about the matter. He admitted that B's manner led him to credit Browning's prejudices more than his statement.

Home did not see fit to follow up Lord Tennyson's invitation to convince him that the séances were authentic. When this invitation came, Home was near the end of his life. Perhaps he no longer cared whom he impressed. More probably, he had had enough of poets.

Browning also condemned Home to Charles Dickens. Dickens, unlike Thackeray, Lord Tennyson, and others Browning tried to influence, agreed with the poet. Dickens was an enemy of spiritualism. This is surprising for two reasons. The first is that he had written one of the most famous ghost stories in English literature, *A Christmas Carol*. The second involves his teenage sister-in-law, Mary Hogarth, of whom he had been especially fond. Her death was a great blow to Dickens, and he thought that her spirit was always near him.

Yet, he echoed Robert Browning in denouncing Home. The big difference between Dickens and Browning was that Browning had seen a Home séance; Dickens had not. In a letter to Mrs. Lynn Linton, a writer who urged him to see Home, Dickens claimed that it was impossible for him to waste time on such things. All séances were conducted, he complained, in places where it was impossible to take precautions against deceit. Secondly, he said that people who saw these séances lied so much that an honest observer was at a disadvantage in telling what really happened. "Mr. Hume, or Home (I rather think he has gone by both names) I take the liberty of regarding as an imposter."

Dickens' attitude irritated Elizabeth Barrett Browning. She said bitingly, "Dickens is so fond of ghost stories, so long as they are impossible!"

Home's quarrel with Brewster and Browning was spread over a number of years, of course, and our story has jumped over much that happened in between in order to present the quarrels together. We will now go back to Ealing just after the Browning séance in July 1855.

8

LOST POWERS AND A FRIENDLY POPE

Browning's attack was a blow to Home, but he quickly recovered from the humiliation of being ordered from Browning's home. He went on vacation with the Rymers to the coast and continued to stay with them until the fall. His health turned bad again, possibly due to the heavy London fogs, which were heavily mixed with coal smoke.

The Rymers' son, who was close to Home's age (twenty-two), suggested a trip to Italy. There was a large colony of British and American expatriates there, including poets, writers, artists, and former diplomats. Mrs. Rymer, concerned over the effects of London fogs on Home's delicate health, paid Home's fare. The two young men were to be house guests of Fanny Trollope, who had a villa in Florence.

The Brownings also had a home in Florence, but they were in Paris when Home arrived. The Florence expatriates were a very gossipy bunch of people and great letter writers. So Elizabeth Barrett Browning learned of

Home's arrival and of his extraordinary success as a medium. Gossip also told her of Home's lack of success in his personal affairs.

Mrs. Browning continued to get a stream of letters about Home. It is chiefly to her own letters, passing along the gossip to her sister and others, that we owe our knowledge of Home's activity in Italy. His own account, of course, paints a more genteel picture. Actually, in his autobiography Home did not say much about himself or his work. Instead he included lengthy quotes from material written by others who told of and praised his accomplishments. His own remarks were a commentary that introduced and explained these quotes.

Of his Italian adventures, Home wrote:

> I remained in Florence till the month of February, 1856, and although some persons there did all they could to injure me by false statements, I was only the more cherished by those who best knew me. . . . The manifestations while I was at Florence were very strong. I remember on one occasion when the Countess ?—— [Orsini] was seated at one of Erard's grand-action pianos, it rose and balanced itself in the air during the whole time she was playing.

The countess, despite this decidedly odd experience, was still skeptical when Home brought her a spelled-out message supposedly from the spirit of her father. She picked up a book from a table and challenged the spirit.

"If you are really the spirit of my father, convince me by writing your name in this book," she said.

She balanced the book on her knees, holding a pencil in her hand. The pencil was gently pulled from her fingers. It moved through the air and quickly scrawled a name across the flyleaf of the book. The countess could see no hand holding the pencil.

She inspected the signature and again challenged the spirit.

"There is a resemblance to my father's writing," she said. "But can you write more distinctly?"

This time the spirit writing took the pencil and again signed his name, adding the words, "My dear daughter—"

The countess made no comment, but the next day she cut the spirit inscription from the book and showed it to an old friend of her father.

"Can you tell who wrote this?" she asked.

"Of course," the man replied. "Your father wrote it. I know his writing well."

"It was written last evening!" the countess replied.

"Impossible!"

"Oh, it is so!" the countess's husband put in.

The man muttered something polite and left hastily. Later he confided to another guest that both the count and the countess were mad!

Home always insisted that he had no power over the spirits. They came to him as they desired. He also insisted that they were *spirits*. Ghosts were something that haunted houses, and he had nothing to do with such evil spirits. However, there were occasions when he did have contact with the old-fashioned haunting type of ghost.

During a party soon after his arrival in Florence, Home was approached by Mrs. Annie Crossman, an Englishwoman, who lived in a very old villa on the outskirts of town.

"Sometimes late at night after I have dismissed my maid, I like to sit or write or read," she told Home. "At such times I am often seized with a strange sense of dread. I can't describe just how I feel at these times, but it is as if I am no longer *alone!*"

"I see," Home replied. "Is there anything else—any sign or sight?"

"I sometime hear rustling noises as if someone was disturbing the bed curtains," she replied. "This noise is always accompanied by a chilliness in the room— something like one may feel if a door is suddenly opened on a cold night."

Mrs. Crossman went on to say that the noises and uneasy feeling intensified after Home arrived in Florence. The medium asked if this feeling and noise happened in any other room of the house.

"I had my bed moved to another room. It was the same," she said. "And it was not just confined to me. My sister had the same feeling and heard the same noises when she visited me."

Home agreed to hold a séance. He left the Trollopes' home to spend three days as Mrs. Crossman's guest. A séance was held the first night in an attempt to discover the source of the noises. Describing the occasion later, the hostess said:

We had scarcely sat a moment at the table, when it began slowly to move about in different directions, generally inclining on the side on which I sat. Presently the movements became more violent. They assumed, if I may use the expression, an angry appearance. We asked if a spirit was present. The table replied by making three movements.

She went on to say, "A high-backed old-fashioned chair, which stood at a little distance from the table was suddenly, and without human contact, drawn close to it, as though some one, in sitting down, had so drawn it. Nothing, however, was visible."

This first séance was inconclusive. Home tried again the following night. There was considerable disturbance. A dagger drew itself from its sheath. The table was lifted in the air and then shoved violently across the room. A bell rang itself. Then Mrs. Crossman reported: "My elbow was violently grasped by a hand, the fingers of which I distinctly saw—they were long, yellow and shining. . . . I spoke gently to the spirit. In answer to my question, the spirit replied that he was unhappy. He promised to return and speak further on the following night."

On the following night the spirit revealed that he had been a renegade monk named Giannana. In some unrevealed way this monk had been involved in a murder or murders, for he said bitterly that he knew too well how to employ a dagger. After unburdening his soul, the spirit promised not to disturb Mrs. Crossman again.

He kept his promise as far as she was concerned. However, after she had sold the villa, the ghost returned to the master bedroom, for this was the place where he had died. In a letter to friends, Mrs. Crossman said the new owners were complaining bitterly about the nocturnal noises.

Home was the social lion of Florence. Everyone sought his attention. His head was turned. He developed an exaggerated sense of his own importance. He quarreled with John Rymer, the young man whose family had paid Home's passage to Italy. In this instance the Florence colony blamed Home, according to letters received by Mrs. Browning in Paris. Arthur Conan Doyle, a strong Home supporter, said that he had seen letters written between Home and young Rymer that showed that Home "had deserted his friend under circumstances which showed inconsistency and ingratitude."

Lord Adare—who had witnessed Home's famous window float in London—years later wrote of Home:

> He had the defects of an emotional character. His vanity was highly developed, perhaps wisely to enable him to hold his own against the ridicule that was then poured out on Spiritualism and everything connected with it. He was liable to fits of great depression and to nervous crises difficult to understand, but he was withal of a simple, kindly, humorous, loving disposition that appealed to me.

Opinion turned sharply against Home in Italy, although he was still sought for his occult powers. Just what he did is difficult to determine, for these Victorian letter writers only hinted at scandals. Mrs. Browning wrote to her sister that Home was forced to leave the Trollope home because of "some failure in his moral character." He was also condemned for staying at the home of a woman who had separated from her husband. He had financial difficulties and was accused of improperly charging a fifty-dollar coat—an expensive item for the time—to the Rymers.

The second Mrs. Home, writing after her husband's death, denied the coat story. She said the whole thing started from a gift of fifty dollars Home made to Mrs. Rymer. She said:

A few years after the séances at Ealing, embarrassments and conduct of others involved Mr. Rymer in absolute ruin. . . . Despairing of finding a position in England, he went to Australia to try his fortune there. His wife and children wished to join him, but lacked the means. Mrs. Rymer wrote to Home entreating him to aid her. This was in the autumn of 1859. On November 1st of that year Mrs. Rymer was able to write Mr. Home a letter now before me:—

"My Dear Dan—I cannot in words express my thanks for your affectionate generosity, which enables me to follow my beloved husband to the new country. . . ."

Mrs. Home's claim that the story of Daniel's imposition upon the Rymers for fifty dollars is rooted in this account sounds very good, except for one thing. Daniel gave Emma Rymer the money for her Australian passage in 1859. The coat incident supposedly happened in 1853.

Home's reputation among the poorer classes of Florence was disastrous. It had only been fifty-seven years since the notorious black magician Cagliostro died in the papal dungeon in Rome. His memory was still very much alive, made much worse than it had actually been by superstition and folklore that had grown up around this great charlatan.

Whispers sped through Florence that Home was another black magician in league with the devil. No one doubted that Home consorted with spirits, but they said he summoned them with forbidden incantations and magical rites.

In January 1856 a high government official warned Home to remain indoors at night and to stay away from lighted or open windows. Home said:

The reason was that some of my enemies had been playing upon the superstitions of the peasantry, telling

them that it was my practice to administer the seven
sacraments of the Catholic Church to toads, in order by
spells and incantations to raise the dead. This had so
enraged and excited them that they were fully bent on
taking my life.

Earlier, in December 1855, there had been an attack on
Home in the streets near the place where he was staying.
At the time it had been put down as a possible robbery
attempt. In light of the official warning Home received
in January, it now seems likely that the attack had been
inspired by superstition.

Home's account of this attack reads:

> I was returning to my rooms late at night, the streets
> being deserted. I observed a man stepping from the
> doorway of the adjoining house. . . . I received a violent
> blow on my left side. The force threw me backward into
> the corner of the doorway. The blow was repeated on my
> stomach, and then another blow on the same place. The
> attempted assassin cried out, "My God! My God!"

The man then turned and ran. Home was so stunned
that it was almost two full minutes before he could
stumble over to a neighboring house to get aid. An
examination showed that the first blow struck a large
house key Home carried in his breast pocket. It deflected
what could have been a fatal blow. Thick folds of his
double-breasted overcoat had stopped the murderous
slash. The third blow penetrated through to his skin, but
the cut was not deep.

Although he was not hurt badly, the attack, added to
his other troubles, increased Home's nervousness. His
health took a turn for the worse. He had irritated so
many who had previously supported him that he was in
danger of starving. Home wrote of this period: "I was

left in Florence without money, and my friends in England having their credulity imposed upon by some scandalmongers, thought I was leading a most dissolute life. They refused to send me even my own money, which I had entrusted to their care."

Though there were plenty of people who thought Home was a fraud, none had been able to prove it. For every disbeliever among the Florence colony of expatriates, there were two believers. But even these believers had turned against him because of his manner. His arrogance and rudeness—in direct contrast to his gentlemanly manner in the United States and England— offended them.

Proof that it was his manner rather than a "dissolute life" that offended his former friends is shown by a letter Elizabeth Barrett Browning wrote her sister Henrietta. Elizabeth and Robert Browning were still in Paris, but letters had kept her as familiar with Home's actions as if she had been in Florence. She had been dismayed by what had been written to her.

In March 1856, John Phipps, brother of Lord Normanby, stopped to see the Brownings on his way to London after a visit to Italy. "He told us . . . about . . . the mystery of iniquity which everybody raved about and nobody distinctly specified." This turned out to be, she added, an enormous amount of exaggeration. "Just as I supposed," she said. "He was blameable, and gave sign of a vulgar yankee nature. But there was nothing at all of the criminal nature which we all supposed here."

Later she was highly pleased to learn that some elaborate schemes to prove Home a fraud had failed. This occurred at the home of Hiram Powers, a noted American sculptor, who lived with his wife in Florence. At a séance at Powers' home, the medium was challenged to

perform with his legs and arms tied. He did so, con-
founding his enemies. Then unknown to Home, they
slipped a man under the drapery of the séance table to
catch him creating the spirit rapping with his foot.
Again they failed to catch him in any type of fraud. On
this occasion, a spirit hand appeared, pulled a chair back
from the table and wrote a message. Hiram Powers
identified the writing as that of his mother.

Home's failing health, his nervous condition, and his
bitter resentment of the treatment he was receiving all
combined to make it extremely difficult for him to continue. So on February 10, 1856, he announced that his
spirit friends told him that the power of communicating
with them would be withdrawn for an entire year.

The spirits had always operated on a high plane and
were apparently resentful of Home's recent actions.
They were punishing him for his lack of humility. Since
he had always lived as the guest of people interested in
his séances, this left him with no means of support.

Fortunately, he had recently met a Polish count and
his family, who had taken an extraordinary interest in
the young medium. The count invited Home to accompany them to Naples and Rome.

"I thought their interest in me arose from the singular
phenomena which they had witnessed in my presence,"
Home said later. "So I informed them that my power had
been taken away from me for a year."

Count Branicka replied that they were interested in
Home as a person as much as for his mediumship. He
renewed his invitation, and Home accepted. His joy at
getting away from the hateful atmosphere of Florence
did much to improve his health.

They spent six weeks in Naples, visiting at one time
the partially excavated ruins of Pompeii. It was sug-

gested to Home that he could prove how true-to-life Bulwer-Lytton's book, *The Last Days of Pompeii,* really was. All he had to do was raise one of the spirits who died there when the city was buried by an eruption of Mount Vesuvius in A.D. 79. Unfortunately, he had no power to contact spirits, he said. Spirits contacted him at their will, and it would—by the spirits' claim—be a year before they would contact him again.

From Naples, Home traveled with Count Branicka and his family to Rome. There was some uneasiness about this. The Catholic Church had always taken a decided opposition to sorcery in any form. The memory of the infamous Cagliostro was still strong in the Eternal City. Many false stories about Home had come from Florence.

Count Branicka, himself a prominent Catholic in Poland, put out the word that Home had lost his spiritual power. The medium would not attempt any séances in Rome. Branicka hurriedly made these statements after a friend in Florence had written Home that Church authorities intended to banish him from Rome.

In Rome events moved swiftly and finally brought Home a personal audience with Pope Pius IX, a very remarkable man. With the loss of his power to talk with spirits, Home was lost himself. "Life seemed to me a blank," he wrote later. He began to read about the history of the Catholic Church. He found many things that coincided with his own experiences, and he took a still deeper interest in the religion. He said that his recent experiences in Florence "of life and its falsity had left an indelible mark on my soul." This caused him to decide on conversion to Catholicism with the intention of entering a monastery, renouncing the world entirely.

He continued his studies in the religion. Then, "After

two or three weeks of serious deliberations on the part of the authorities, it was decided that I should be received as a member of the church."

Soon after his confirmation, Home was received by the Pope. Pius IX took some time with Home, questioning him about his past life. Home detailed his early psychic experiences. His Holiness listened quietly, asked probing questions, but made no comment. However, when Home made a remark about his faith in the spirit world, Pius pointed to a crucifix, saying, "My child, it is upon what is on that table that we place our faith."

At the end of the audience Home remarked that he expected to visit Paris in company with the Branicka family. Pius suggested that he take Father de Ravignan, a highly regarded French priest, as his confessor and teacher. He gave Home a silver medal at their parting.

At this point, it seemed that Home had turned his back forever on the life of a medium. His intention was to seclude himself in a monastic life for the rest of his days. He had decided upon a French monastery and wanted to learn the language before taking his vows.

However, the call of the occult proved too strong.

9

RETURNING SPIRITS AND AN ANGRY EMPRESS

Home arrived with Count Branicka in Paris in June 1856. He immediately contacted Father Xavier de Ravignan, who had received a communication from the Vatican asking him to counsel the new convert. Father de Ravignan took a great interest in the young man and spent much time with Home. He seems also to have helped Home find lodgings after the Branicka family returned to Poland, leaving the medium destitute in Paris.

Mrs. Browning was still in Paris when Home arrived, but did not meet him. She did note his arrival in one of her letters and expressed worry about what would happen if Robert Browning happened to meet Home. Browning assured her that, despite how much he detested Home, he would be "meek as a lamb" if they should meet accidentally. This feared meeting did not take place, and the Brownings soon left to return to their villa in Florence. Elizabeth asked all her Parisian friends to keep her posted on news of Home's activities in the French capital.

There wasn't much to report, since he was giving no séances. At one point she received a message that Home was near death. This was exaggerated, but he was ill. A French doctor advised him to go to a warmer climate because of his lung trouble. Home was unable to do so because there was no one to pay the bill.

As the year of lost power passed, speculation was high in Paris about its possible return. February 10, 1857, was the day set by the spirits when they took away the power in Florence. The speculation reached Father de Ravignan, who discussed it with Home. Home insisted, as he always did, that he had no power to call any spirits. They came and went at their own desire, working through him only when it so suited their fancy. He denied to Father de Ravignan that he had promised the Pope to avoid all future spirit manifestations. "I could not have made any such promise," Home said. "Nor did His Holiness ask for any such promise to be made."

As the end of the year of suspension approached, Home became increasingly nervous. De Ravignan thought this was due to worry about being bothered by the spirits. He assured Daniel that, now that the young man was a member of the Catholic Church, the spirits could not trouble him again.

On the night of February 10, 1857, Home was ill in bed. He was awake, unable to sleep. Precisely after the clock struck midnight, he heard loud rappings in the room. His spirit friends had returned. A spirit hand was placed on his feverish brow. He heard a voice say, "Be of good cheer, Daniel, you will soon be well." A few minutes later, Home went to sleep. He reports:

I awakened in the morning feeling more refreshed than I had done for a long time. I wrote to the Pére de Ravignan, telling him what had occurred. The same afternoon he came to see me. During our conversation loud rappings were heard on the ceiling and on the floor. As he was about to give me his benediction before leaving, loud raps came on the bedstead. He left me without expressing any opinion on the subject of the phenomena.

The same day a messenger arrived from Napoleon III, the emperor of France, inquiring about the return of Home's spiritualistic powers. He invited Home to the palace on the thirteenth. Home agreed, but did not tell his father confessor.

When Home arrived at the palace, he found the drawing room jammed with people. He refused as politely as he could to give a séance. He explained that a large crowd upset his spirit friends. He suggested a maximum of eight people. Empress Eugénie, consort of Napoleon III, was outraged. She left the room, giving Home a withering glare as she left.

The emperor had had much experience with charlatans and frauds. In addition he was an amateur magician. He smiled faintly as he agreed to exclude all but eight people from the séance. He expected to expose Home without any difficulty.

Louis Napoleon was the nephew of Napoleon I. After his famous uncle had been defeated and sent into exile by the British, Louis spent a number of years in exile himself. He was then involved in a revolution attempt in Italy, and twice tried to overthrow the French government. He turned reformer and in 1844 wrote a book in which he proposed that the French government act to end all poverty in the nation. He returned to France in 1848, when the revolution of that year brought the Second Republic into being. He was elected to the French Assembly and then became Assembly president, receiving over 5 million votes out of a possible 7.5 million. He quickly consolidated his power and in 1852 proclaimed himself Emperor of France.

Home did not say much about this séance. *Harper's Weekly*, the American magazine, had this account in the September 12, 1857, issue:

> When they were assembled the spirit of the older Napoleon was envoked, and in reply to questions communicated facts which thunderstruck all who were present, the Emperor alone excepted.
>
> "Bah!" said his Majesty, "a careful study of my uncle's writing might enable any clever person to forge these answers." [Apparently the demonstration had been an example of spirit writing, which Home had done before.]
>
> "Would your Majesty grant me a private audience for a quarter of an hour?" asked the young medium.
>
> "Certainly," was the smiling reply. "Come tomorrow morning at ten. We shall see if we can not exorcise these spirits."
>
> What passed at the private interview is not known. It has been surmised that the spirit who was evoked on that occasion was that of Napoleon's brother, whose death is clouded in so much mystery. From the fact that the Emperor fell into a deep melancholy when the "medium" was gone, it has been conjectured that his Majesty did not find his exorcising operations a laughing matter.
>
> Public rumor, indeed, asserts that on the following day Napoleon offered a million [francs] to Home for "his secret." The young man informed his Majesty that he knew no more of the secret than anyone else. Home surmised that his supernatural powers were due to his

infirm health and approaching death, as he had noticed that the raps increased when he was worst, and decreased in number and intensity as he got better.

There is a basic difference between this account and another of the same séance. The second account makes no mention of Home having a second private interview with Louis Napoleon. It claims that the emperor became so interested in Home's exhibition that he interrupted to exclaim: "Her Majesty must see this!"

Napoleon sent for Eugénie, who came with ill grace. At the suggestion of Napoleon, Prince Joachim Murat bent under the table to hold Home's feet. As an amateur conjuror himself and a friend of the famous magician Robert-Houdin, Napoleon knew about the art of trickery.

The table began to rock. Napoleon spoke to Murat, who shook his head. The rocking was certainly not caused by Home's feet, as had been so often claimed. Then something tugged at Empress Eugénie's gown. She looked down quickly and appeared startled when she saw nothing to cause it.

Home then suggested that she put her hand under the table. "Do not be surprised or startled if another hand should take hers." She did as bidden. A hand touched hers. She cried, "It is my father's hand!" Louis Napoleon moved quickly over beside her. He reached under the table himself. He also identified the hand as belonging to the empress' father. They identified it by a crooked finger. The hand felt as if it were wearing a silk glove.

From this moment on, Empress Eugénie was as ardent a believer in Home as Elizabeth Barrett Browning. A few weeks later, the Paris correspondent of *Harper's Weekly* spread this gossip to the United States:

One of the most ardent proselytes of Home is the Empress. She had him constantly at her apartments, and was so intimate with him that the wicked tongue of Paris was soon busy with scandal. . . . At all events, the Emperor at last disapproved of his wife's association with the dangerous wizard, and forbade her to see him more. It is understood that he still vaticinates for her benefit through the aid of her ladies of honor.

Harper's Weekly, a distinguished magazine published from 1857 until 1916, is a gold mine for researchers into the activities of its time. However, it was not always accurate. In the case of Home, the reports were completely founded upon gossip, and gossip, although often based upon some degree of truth, is seldom the whole story or the true story. In this case, Louis Napoleon was present at all séances given to Eugénie, and he did not forbid her to see Home.

In fact, the entire French court flocked around him. He was invited to royal parties and to the most fashionable homes. His unhappy experience in Florence had taught him a lesson he never forgot. Now his manners were perfect, his rudeness and arrogance had been put aside. He moved quietly and with dignity through the often raucous social world of the Second Empire.

Home's return to séances did not please his father confessor at all. Home tried to reason with him, reiterating that he was not responsible for the "visitations" and, indeed, that he considered them a blessing from God, which he dared not ignore. But Father de Ravignan would not listen. "Do as I bid you," he ordered Home, "or bear the consequences."

Home had always been sincere in his religious beliefs. Even as a child he had read his Bible daily. There is nothing to indicate that he was not equally sincere in joining the Catholic Church. However, he now found himself in a position where the Church conflicted with his lifework.

From the time his aunt's table rocked the harder when she placed a Bible upon it, Home had believed that there was nothing in spiritualism that conflicted with Christianity. Still, not trusting his own judgment, he went to a friend, Count Alexander de Komar, seeking advice. The count suggested another confessor and asked a famous clergyman to give Home advice. This man came, listened to some rappings, and saw a table move without visible means. Impressed, he recommended that Home see a new spiritual adviser and recommended another priest.

But the new confessor soon gave up on Home, too, and the young man made his decision: His life was to be devoted to spiritualism. He never formally left the Church, and later when he married in the Russian Orthodox Church, he insisted on having a second Catholic ceremony. However, Daniel was never again a practicing member of the Church. The poor boy who had achieved his ambition of walking with kings and nobles had no intention of giving up the gift that made it possible.

Many memoirs left by famous people of the French Second Empire tell of Home. Princess Caroline Murat said that to tell all she saw of Daniel's spirits would be impossible and unbelievable to readers who had not been there. She told of evenings at the Paris opera followed by late suppers and concluding with delightful séances with Home. "Unseen hands played the accordion or piano—tables covered with glass and plate lifted suddenly over our heads—noise as if every window and mirror in the room was ringing with sounds that told us Home was coming, was in the house," she wrote.

Naturally enough, Home made more enemies. The old stories of Brewster and Browning were retold. Michael Faraday, whose work led to the electric generator and electric motor, blasted spiritualism in general and Home in particular. A statement of Senator James Shields to the United States Congress was widely quoted both in Paris and London. Shields said:

> The prevalence of this delusion at this age of the world, among any considerable portion of our citizens, must originate, in my opinion, in a defective system of education, or in a partial derangement of the mental faculties. . . . I have said enough to show the truth of [Edmund] Burke's beautiful aphorism: "The credulity of dupes is as inexhaustible as the invention of knaves."

When they could not find any other way to attack Home, reporters invented stories to make him look ridiculous. One of these was the famous "Socrates story." This invention originally appeared in the English paper *The Court Reporter*, under the head, "Singular and Successful Hoax on the Spiritualists." The Paris correspondent for *Harper's Weekly* copied the story and added some changes.

The *Harper's* account claimed that Home raised the spirit of Socrates at a séance attended by Marshal Baraguay d'Hilliers (identified only as "the general").

> "This is very well, Monsieur Home," the general said. "You can make Socrates talk, but can you make him appear before us?"
>
> "Certainly not," replied the medium.
>
> "Oh, you have something to learn, then. I can." . . .

The company, of course, burst into exclamations. The gallant officer, with seeming modesty, tried to excuse himself, alleging that he had learned the art of raising the dead among the Arabs. . . . Feigning to yield, he requested Home to evoke the spirit of Socrates by his method.

The raps declared that the philosopher was there.

"Now," said the general, "shade of Socrates, I command thee to appear!"

There was a dead silence for a moment. The gas fell [meaning the gaslight dimmed]. The room began to look weird. The ladies trembled. All eyes were fixed on the door, where, to the general consternation, presently appeared the well-known figure of the Athenian sage with his snub nose, and goggle eyes, and Greek dress.

"I am here," said he, in a sepulchral voice.

The ladies screamed. The specter slowly entered the room, treading lightly as became a ghost, and walked straight to Home, who stood tottering near the mantelpiece. Fixing his eyes upon Home, the spirit murmured in a hollow voice,

"Man, why dost thou disturb my slumbers in the grave?"

With a fearful shriek Home fell, bleeding from the mouth and nostrils. The apparition terrified him beyond bearing. He who believed that he communicated with the spirits daily almost died of fright at the sight of a trick which almost any man in the world would have seen through!

Concerning this story, Home wrote: "The whole [story of the practical joke] was a fabrication, for at that time I had never even seen either of the two gentlemen who were said to be actors in it."

Even wilder tales were circulated about Home. One claimed that Daniel cried like a baby and groveled at the feet of Father de Ravignan, begging forgiveness for consorting with the devil. According to another story,

Home was riding in a railway carriage and fell into conversation with a fellow passenger. Not recognizing Home, the man began to talk fearfully about the spiritualist, and, Home asked him what he would do if he found himself in a carriage with his bugaboo.

"I'd jump right out the window," said the passenger.

Home rose and lowered the compartment window. He then bowed courteously and said with an amused smile, "I am D. D. Home. *Bon voyage!*"

French and foreign politicians took a great interest in Home because he was being received by the emperor. For this reason, he was under surveillance by the French secret police to ensure that none of the politicians tried to take advantage of Home's intimacy with the royal pair.

There was even a story that the emperor's cabinet wanted Napoleon to ban Home from the country, lest foreign diplomats get the idea that ghosts were helping make imperial decisions. This rumor was "proved" when Home suddenly left France for the United States on March 20, 1857. Even Princess Murat thought that Home had been banished.

Actually, he was returning to the United States to get his sister Caroline, whom Empress Eugénie had offered to educate in a Paris convent. No one believed this story, which was the truth. But many did believe a particularly vicious tale that Home had fled Paris to escape being imprisoned for theft of a large sum of money. This story literally accompanied Home to America, for a New York *Herald* correspondent rushed it down to the port and got it aboard the same ship on which Home was sailing. The story was published soon after the medium arrived in New York.

When questioned about the "theft," Home said only

that the *Herald* was a paper "better known for its un-
truthfulness than otherwise." He added that he had his
return ticket to Paris in his pocket. He could hardly
expect to return if he had indeed stolen $150,000 in
French francs.

There was another story that a beautiful girl had killed
herself in Italy for love of the handsome medium. Then
the New York *Herald* quoted a French paper:

> Napoleon III sent Mr. Home, the American spirit-
> rapper, from France because the Empress was so much
> affected that the Emperor dreaded the continuance of the
> diabolical scenes. The Empress's ladies of honor were
> equally excited and could talk of nothing but Home. It is
> said that Home was quartered in the royal household
> and paid at the rate of 40,000 pounds [about $200,000
> then] per year.

The only true statement in the story was that the
empress and her ladies-in-waiting were excited over
Home. He was not sent away by Napoleon. He was paid
nothing by the royal family, although other friends did
furnish him a place to live. Sometime during his Paris
stay, a woman Home had never met died and left him a
legacy worth about $1,200 a year.

Reporters tried to tie Home to other famous mediums
of his day. They asked him about Katie and Margaretta
Fox, the Hydesville girls who started modern spiritualism. He denied ever meeting them.

Unsatisfied, they tried to get him to accompany them
to a public test being arranged for another young girl
almost as famous as the Fox sisters. She was Cora Scott
Hatch. Cora had seen Katie Fox at a séance in New York,
and at the age of ten became a medium herself. She
married her manager, a man named Hatch, when she

Cora Scott Hatch had a large following as a spiritualist, but failed to impress Home. Photo from Emma Hardinge's *Modern American Spiritualism*.

was fifteen. A dark, brooding man, he and a minister of the gospel stood on each side of Cora—as if to protect her from the spirits—during her séances. She was considered to be the most beautiful medium of her time, and surviving pictures support the belief. She had large, soulful eyes set in an ivory skin framed by shoulder-length blond curls. She was then seventeen years old.

An irreverent reporter from the *Herald* cast doubt on her age:

> She is a slender girl who apparently has not been seventeen—the advertised age—for more than three or four years. A profusion of sunny ringlets and a fresh youthful complexion gives her an almost childish air. . . . [She] gives an impression of sorrowful submission to the powers that be, which was heightened by the inexorable scowl of a powerful man who appears as Mr. Hatch, and who with the Reverend S. B. Brittan accompanies her to the platform.

Cora Hatch gave lectures while in a spirit trance. One of them was about life in the spirit world. She claimed life there was lived on several levels, depending upon one's faith. Since this was at odds with Home's account of his own journey into the world of spiritland, the reporters wanted him to join the group testing Mrs. Hatch. Some of Cora's lectures were strongly anti-Catholic. Home still professed to be a Catholic despite the Church's opposition to his spiritualism. The reporters hoped to use this religious conflict to get Home to expose the pretty medium.

Although he hinted that many mediums were fakes and should be exposed, he refused to join in the tests. In the company of a discreet friend, he did slip into the hall to witness one of Cora's exhibitions—they could not be called séances. The friend expressed the opinion that it was a shame Cora was married to "that ugly brute Hatch." Pretty Cora and handsome Daniel would have made a fine couple. Home replied quietly that a medium wife was the last thing in the world he wanted. He did not explain why he felt this way.

Although most papers attacked Home unmercifully, some treated him more fairly. A Hartford, Connecticut, newspaper wrote, "We regard [Home] as the most remarkable man living. No man who has not witnessed what is done in Home's presence can claim a right to give an opinion of Spiritualism."

10

BRICKBATS, FLOWERS, AND WEDDING BELLS

When Daniel Home left the United States for Europe in 1855, there was strong public opinion against spiritualism. It was even worse when he returned in 1857.

After the Fox sisters originated spirit-rapping as a means of communicating with the dead, thousands of mediums sprang up all over the country. Many, perhaps, were sincere, but the majority were frauds or so badly deluded that they were a public menace.

One group used spiritualism as an excuse for immoral conduct. Another claimed the Bible a myth. Numerous personal tragedies were reported as a direct result of consort with mediums. Several separate cases were reported of people killing themselves because a medium pictured the spirit world as better than this world.

One man attacked his mother with a hatchet because she derided spiritualism. He claimed he was only trying to open her head so some sense could get in. Another killed himself because a medium told him that his dead fiancée was calling for him.

Many of these cases happened to people of a hysterical or unbalanced nature, of course, but more sensible people were also affected. Judge John W. Edmonds of the New York Supreme Court, one of the first important people to embrace spiritualism, was forced to resign from the bench. He had been accused of permitting the spirits to influence his judgments.

The judge set up a private practice and strongly supported spiritualism to the day of his death. More tragic was the case of John B. Fairbanks, a noted inventor and editor of the *Scientific American* magazine, one of the most respected scientific publications.

Fairbanks had been greatly influenced by Dr. Robert Hare, professor of chemistry at the University of Pennsylvania, who delivered a paper on spiritualism to the American Association for the Advancement of Science in August 1856. Hare reminded his audience of renowned scientists that many of the great discoveries of science had at first been condemned as frauds.

Fairbanks had earlier lost a beloved sister. After listening to Hare, he made an appointment to see Margaretta Fox. He came away from his first séance absolutely convinced that he had indeed conversed with his dead sister. Then in November 1856—four months before Home arrived back in New York—Fairbanks went to an empty room of a hotel. He spent several hours talking to himself. Finally he opened the window and threw himself out. He was killed in the fall. The coroner's report said that Fairbanks believed that he would join his sister in the spirit world.

George Templeton Strong, a noted lawyer, was alarmed at the spread of spiritualism. He wrote:

> I am surprised that so many of my friends regard the prevalence of this delusion with so much indifference. It

is surely one of the most startling events that have occurred for centuries . . . A new Revelation, hostile to that
of the Church and the Bible, finding acceptance on the
authority of knocking ghosts and oscillating tables . . .

Oliver Wendell Holmes, the distinguished author of
The Autocrat of the Breakfast Table, also joined the attack
on mediums. The New York *Tribune* quoted him as
saying, "While some are crying against [spiritualism] as
a delusion of the Devil, and some are laughing at it as an
hysteric folly, and some are getting angry with it as a
trick of interested or mischievous persons, Spiritualism
is quietly undermining the traditional ideas of the future state which have been and are still accepted. . . ."

In contrast to the money-hungry, often irreligious
mediums who were causing such criticism throughout
the United States, Home always fitted his spiritual beliefs into the basic frame of orthodox religion. He refused to be drawn into the current controversy and
turned down all attempts to get him to give séances
during his stay in the United States. When a group
offered him $10,000 (a very large sum for 1857), he re-
fused to answer their letter. He had similarly turned
down a group in France.

Home and his sister sailed for Paris in May. After
placing her in the Sacred Heart Convent, he resumed his
work. Elizabeth Barrett Browning, after picking up gossip from her many correspondents in Paris, wrote her
sister that Daniel was again holding séances in the
palace. She claimed that he had materialized the ghostly
figures of a man and a woman whom the audience
recognized. Several of the witnesses fainted.

In late May, Home went with the royal party to a resort
outside Paris. There they were joined by the Grand

Duke Constantine of Russia. This meeting would later lead to Home's first marriage. Then Home added another king to his list of royal patrons. Maximilian II of Bavaria, a rather nervous man of advanced age, arrived for a visit.

Home was privileged to ride back to Paris on the imperial train. In the second series of his memoirs Home tells us that the spirits, being in a playful mood, frightened King Maximilian so badly that he ran to his compartment and did not come out until the train reached Paris.

What happened was that the party was in the parlor car of the train when a grand duchess cried, "Come quickly, Mr. Home! The table is moving!"

King Maximilian turned and saw the table slowly moving toward him. Home wrote in his memoirs, "I shall never forget the downright look of terror on the [king's] face, as he first looked at that table moving without visible aid. . . . At last the table rose in the air at least half a foot. This was too much. The king, making for the door, vanished, and was no more visible until we reached Paris."

Soon after returning to Paris, Home became seriously ill. Empress Eugénie, becoming alarmed, sent her personal physician to treat Daniel. The doctor, Eugene Barthez, detested Home and all other spiritualists. During the treatment, Home went into a trance. The doctor brought him out of it by sarcastically remarking, "Enough of this, Monsieur Home. I do not believe in spirits!"

Home's illness was real enough, and he decided to go to Italy in search of a warmer climate. This was surprising, after his miserable experience there before going to Paris. However, his old friend, Countess Orsini, had written, urging him to come.

He had no sooner left Paris than his enemies started an ugly rumor that he had been arrested and was in a French jail. One Paris paper even went so far as to publish an interview with a man who claimed he had carried Home to the prison.

As soon as this libel was cleared up, Home received another shock. Friends in Paris sent him a theater program that read:

At the Great Theater, Thursday, 1st of April, 1858, Commencing at Eight O'clock, American Séance of Spiritualism, by Mr. Home.
Programme: The Vision Experience of Mr. Home, and the Miraculous Angel . . . Productions of Visions Asked for by the Audience . . .
Mr. Home, who has had the honor to go through his experiences before His Majesty, the Emperor, invites the Doctors of Philosophy and others, also Surgeons, etc., etc., to sit near him on the stage to satisfy themselves as to the truth of the curious phenomena which he has the honor to present to the public. Chairs will be arranged for that purpose.

This was not the first time Home had been impersonated. As usual he reacted with rage, writing his friends in Paris to expose the fraud. He had always kept himself above professional mediumship and did not want to be associated in any way with taking money for spiritualistic work. Strangely, he did not condemn other mediums for accepting money. He said he would not do so as long as ministers of the gospel accepted salaries. Everyone had to live in some manner.

Home traveled through Italy. He had lost his power because of his illness, he said as an excuse to avoid giving séances while in Rome.

While in Rome, Home's previous friendship with the

Russian Grand Duke Constantine in Paris got him an invitation to dine with the Count Gregoire de Koucheleff. Home pleaded his inability to perform, but the Countess de Koucheleff replied they wanted him to come anyway. The family had heard a great deal about him from Russian friends in Paris as well as from Elizabeth Barrett Browning, whom the countess also knew.

In the course of the evening the countess introduced Home to her teenage sister, an extremely lovely girl who was the daughter of a former general in the Russian army.

Home wrote: "A strange impression came over me at once, and I knew she was to be my wife."

At the midnight supper, Daniel was seated between the girl, Alexandrina (Sacha) de Kroll, and her sister, the Countess de Koucheleff. Sacha teasingly told Daniel, "Mr. Home, you will be married before the end of the year!"

"Why do you say that?" he asked. Her words oddly reminded him of his impression when he first saw her that here was his future wife.

"In Russia we have a superstition that when a person sits at a table between two sisters he has just met he will be married before the year passes."

Home smiled, but did not reply. In his memoirs he says that the superstition was true. "In twelve days we were partially engaged, and awaiting only the consent of her mother."

Their engagement was announced at another party given by the countess. While the rest of the guests were dancing, Home was seated with Sacha when the subject of his spiritualistic gifts came up between them for the first time.

Home's account of it reads:

> She turned to me and abruptly said, "Do tell me all about spirit-rapping, for you know I don't believe in it."
>
> I said to her, "Mademoiselle, I trust you will ever bear in mind that I have a mission entrusted to me. It is a great and a holy one. I cannot speak with you about a thing which you have not seen, and therefore cannot understand. I can only say that it is a great truth."
>
> The tears came welling into her eyes, and laying her hand in mine she said, "If your mission can bring comfort to those less happy than ourselves, or be in any way a consolation to mankind, you will ever find me ready and willing to do all I can to aid you in it."
>
> She was true to this noble sentiment to the last moment of her short life, and she is still my great comfort and sustainer since we have separated in this earthly sphere. She was my own true loving wife for, oh! too short a period for my happiness here.

Since Sacha was a member of the Russian nobility, permission for the wedding had to be obtained from the czar. Arrangements were made for the wedding to be held in St. Petersburg. Sacha went back to Russia to wait for Home's arrival. He had to go to Scotland to obtain his birth certificate, and then stopped in Paris to get Alexandre Dumas to accompany him to Russia. Dumas was to serve as Home's godfather at the Russian Orthodox ceremony.

Dumas, fat, bombastic, and enormously egotistical, was the author of *The Three Musketeers, The Count of Monte Cristo,* and other novels whose fame has endured to this day. Dumas turned out so many books that he was accused of hiring hack writers to produce them under his name. A story current in Paris at the time claims that a friend enthusiastically praised Dumas' latest book, calling it a masterpiece. "Really?" the writer replied. "Then I must read it someday!"

Dumas was fascinated by the character of Cagliostro, the mystic charlatan who created such a stir in Paris in the late eighteenth century. He had written a book using Cagliostro as a character. He was similarly attracted to Daniel Home, and the two were often seen together when Home was in Paris.

Their friendship was all the more strange because Dumas did not take Home's spiritualism seriously. One account claims that Dumas considered Home a reincarnation of Cagliostro, which, of course, would make Home a prince of imposters. The second Mrs. Home, in her book, *Life and Mission of Home*, says, "Dumas, who never took life seriously, could not accept Home's manifestations as matter for serious consideration. This . . . was more disagreeable to Home than any skepticism, and explains the statement made by Dumas that Home accused him of putting the spirits to flight."

In one of his books Dumas included a sketch of Home's life which Daniel had given him. Mrs. Home says that Dumas "could not resist the temptation to re-touch it. There are natures to which veracity is impossible, and history as treated by Dumas becomes fiction, biography becomes romance. Home, who had expected nothing else, laughed heartily. . . ."

Even so, it was this clown on the stage of life that Home chose for his godfather at the wedding. It must have been because of a genuine liking for Dumas. The writer's romantic style was not appreciated by the fun-loving people of the Second Empire and his popularity had dropped alarmingly.

Home and Dumas went to Russia in June, where they stayed at the estate of Count Koucheleff. Alexander II immediately sent for Home, but the medium excused himself with the claim that he was not in power. The czar replied that this made no difference, but still Home very uncharacteristically refused the invitation.

Shortly after this, governmental red tape threatened to postpone the wedding. Home suddenly found that he was back in power and hastily sent word to the Russian ruler that he could now accept the royal invitation. Instead of being angry, Alexander was amused. He invited Home to spend a week in the royal palace in St. Petersburg. The medium accepted, to the disgust of Dumas, who was not invited. Mrs. Home quotes the writer as saying, "Oh, well, there are other crowned heads in Europe, but there is only one Alexandre Dumas!"

The czar cut the red tape, giving his permission for the wedding along with a diamond ring as a wedding present. The wedding of Daniel and Sacha was held on August 1, 1858, first with a Russian Orthodox ceremony and then, at Home's request, a second Catholic ceremony.

The wedding was a brilliant affair. The only untoward incident was furnished by Dumas. According to Mrs. Home's account:

> At the marriage, it was necessary for Dumas to give his name. On being asked for it, he responded briefly, "Dumas." The official repeated the question.
> "Dumas!" replied the illustrious owner of that name more loudly than before.
> "But your Christian name, Monsieur Dumas?"
> "Alexandre— Is there another Alexandre Dumas in the world?" demanded the outraged author.

The young couple traveled through Russia on their honeymoon, staying with various friends, some very highly placed. Among them was Count Alexis Tolstoi, a poet and relative of the famous writer Leo Tolstoi. The Grand Duke Constantine, brother of the czar, who had first met Home in Paris, also remained a staunch supporter of the young medium.

After her first questions on the evening they became engaged, Sacha did not again inquire about Daniel's spiritualistic work. Then, a short time after their marriage, she was introduced to spiritualism on her own accord. Home's account of this read:

> My wife being in a sound quiet sleep, I saw the spirit of my mother come into the room. She was followed by one I had never known on earth, but I knew to be my wife's father. My impression was one of relief that my wife was asleep. Thus she would not see what I feared would frighten her.
>
> My surprise was therefore great on hearing her say, "Daniel there is some one in the room with us. It is your mother, and near her stands my father. She is very beautiful, and I am not afraid."
>
> Her actions, however, betrayed a certain shrinking, for she turned to the side of the bed where I lay, trembling violently. The spirits now disappeared, but loud rappings were heard in and about the room, and our questions were answered. This was my wife's first introduction to anything of the kind.

Hereafter Sacha took part in spirit rapping with her husband, but never in public. Her part was only asking questions, which the spirits answered with raps. The birth of their son on May 8, 1959, also tended to make spiritualism a family affair with the Homes. The child was born during a snowstorm in St. Petersburg. Home wrote:

A few hours after his birth, his mother, the nurse and I heard for several hours the warbling of a bird as if singing over him. Also that night, and for two or three nights afterwards, a bright starlike light, which was clearly visible from the partial darkness of the room, appeared several times directly over the child's head. It remained there for several moments, and then slowly moved in the direction of the door, where it disappeared.

This was also seen by each of us at the same time. The light was more condensed than those which have been so often seen in my presence upon previous and subsequent occasions. It was brighter and more distinctly globular.

I do not believe that the light came through my mediumship, but rather through that of the child, who had manifested on several occasions the present of the gift. I do not like to allude to such a matter, but as there are more strange things in Heaven and earth than are dreamt of, even in my philosophy, I do not feel myself at liberty to omit stating, that during the latter part of my wife's pregnancy, we thought it better that she should not join in séances. It was found that whenever the rappings occurred in the room, a simultaneous movement of the child was distinctly felt, perfectly in unison with the sounds.

When there were three sounds, three movements were felt, and so on. When five sounds were heard, which is generally the call for the alphabet, she felt the five internal movements. She would frequently, when we were mistaken in the letter, correct us from what the child indicated.

The child, who was named Gregoire for his uncle, later showed other signs of mediumship. Home took his family to Paris in August 1859. Here he experienced again one of his periodic losses of power. One evening in November, he left their chateau for a visit with some friends. When he returned, Sacha told him that she and the baby's nurse had heard loud raps upon the ceiling. Later these changed and seemed to come from the walls and then from a table in the room.

The noise was obviously spiritual, but spirits are not strong enough (according to spiritualism) to manifest themselves. They can do so only through the mediumship of certain people who have spiritual power. "But who was the medium here?" Sacha asked.

"The child," Home replied.

Child mediums, of course, were nothing new. After all, Katie Fox was eleven years old when her questions to the Hydesville knocker ushered in the age of spiritualism. But Home's claim of mediumship for an unborn child first and then again when Gregoire was six months old is unique.

At first Home had definite intentions of developing his son into a medium, but he later changed his mind. In questioning the spirits, he said, he was told that "the atmosphere which they made use of was necessary for [the child's] physical development in the natural world." However, once when a woman at one of his séances claimed that Home had resorted to trickery, he smiled and offered to have his baby son act as the medium for her. She was horrified at the thought of a baby medium and hastily changed the subject.

Ever restless, Home took his family to England. The controversy with Brewster and the angry libels of Robert Browning had done Daniel no injury. The tales of his triumphs in Paris and Russia and an audience with the queen of the Netherlands were on everybody's lips. His old friends and many new ones rushed to honor Home and his lovely young wife.

Home continued to accept invitations to stay with various families, but he was no longer dependent upon charity. Sacha was an heiress. They took a suite in Cox's Hotel and lived in proper style.

Now that the necessity of finding his daily bread was lifted, Home spread his gifts more widely. His power, lost in France, returned in late November after his arrival in London. He writes, "I began to hold séances as usual, and continued to do so until the 24th of July [1860]. During this time, the manifestations were seen and investigated by persons of all ranks and classes, from statesmen down to those in humble life."

This did not mean that Home had lost his snobbish hunger for noble company. He was now intent upon building his reputation. He moved much more in lower levels so that his gifts would be more than just hearsay among people outside the nobility. This was the first time he had done this since he left the United States five years before.

Home was riding the crest of his fame. His enemies were temporarily stilled. But this was to be short-lived. A new storm broke around him in August 1860. Triggered by William Makepeace Thackeray, it caused a flood of condemnation to batter the famous author.

11

FLOATING BODIES AND FIRE TRICKS

Thackeray never publicly acknowledged being a spiritualist, but he was known to be very much interested in the occult. During his lecture tour of the United States in the 1850's, he witnessed séances by the Fox sisters and Daniel Home, among others. He also attended séances held by Home in England.

Thackeray was editor of the *Cornhill Magazine*, a widely read publication. In the August 1860 issue he published an anonymously written article produced by a journalist named Robert Bell. The idea for the article was said to have been Thackeray's, but for political reasons he did not wish to write it himself, and commissioned Bell to do it instead.

The article was published under the title "Stranger than Fiction." It told of Bell's experiences at a Home séance and it included this defiant statement: "It is not a satisfactory answer to those who have seen such things, to say that they are impossible; *since, in such cases, it is evident that the impossibility of a thing does not prevent it happening."*

In a typical séance of the 1850's, the group sat around a circular table, lightly touching the top with their fingertips.

Bell attended several séances before he wrote his story. He admitted that he had heard about tables moving during these meetings, and had been positive that the movement was caused by some members pressing hard with their hands. He found this was not so.

We barely touched the table with the tips of our fingers. . . . My friends kindly gratified my request to avoid resting the slightest weight on the table. We held our hands pointing downward, with merely the nails touching the wood. . . . Presently we had conclusive proof that the vivacity of the table did not require any help from us. . . .

On the first occasion when I experienced the effect I am about to describe, there were five persons in the room. In other places where it occurred subsequently there were seven or more. The architecture of the houses in each case was wholly dissimilar. . . . We were seated at a table at which some singular phenomena, accompanied by loud knocks on the walls and floor, had just occurred, when we became conscious of a strange vibration that palpitated through the entire room.

We listened and watched attentively. The vibrations grew stronger and stronger. It was palpably under our feet. Our chairs shook, and the floor trembled violently. . . . Every person present was equally affected by it on each occasion when it occurred. To produce such a result by machinery might be possible if the introduction of the machinery itself were possible. . . .

Presently the table rises with a slight jerk. It steadily mounts till it attains such a height as to render it necessary for the company to stand up, in order still to be able to keep their hands with ease in contact with the surface.

As there are some present who have not witnessed this movement before, a desire is expressed to examine the floor. A gentleman goes under the table for this purpose.

The investigator, of course, found nothing. The table was not the four-legged variety. It was round on the surface, with the tabletop supported by a round pillar that terminated in three claws of carved wood that spread out to support weight. A tablecloth came down about a foot around the tabletop. After the table rose in the air about a foot, it settled down again with a very slow motion. Bell said it touched down with a "dreamy softness that renders its touch almost imperceptible." Then the table began to tilt:

The table rears itself up on one side until the surface forms an inclined plane, at an angle of about 45°. In this

attitude it stops. According to ordinary experience everything on the table must slide off, or topple over. But
nothing stirs. The vase of flowers, the books, the little
ornaments are as motionless as if they were fixed in their
places.

We agree to take away our hands, to throw up the ends
of the [table] cover, so as to leave the entire round pillar
and claws exposed. We also agree to remove our chairs to
a little distance, that we may have a more complete
command of a phenomenon, which in its marvelous
development at least, is, I believe, new to us all.

Our withdrawal makes no difference whatever. We
now see distinctly on all sides the precise pose of the
table, which looks, like the Leaning Tower of Pisa, as if it
must inevitably tumble over. . . .

A wish is whispered for a still more conclusive display. . . . The desire is at once complied with. The table
leans more and more out of the perpendicular. Two of
the three claws are high above the floor. Finally, the
whole structure stands on the extreme tip of one claw,
fearfully overbalanced.

Bell's account then turned to the self-playing accordion. While some earlier accounts of this claimed the
playing was bad, Bell was lavish in his praise of the
musical quality: "The notes swelled in some of the bold
passages. The sound rolled through the room with an
astounding reverberation; then gently subsiding, sank
into a strain of divine tenderness. . . ." Bell claimed that
the playing could not have been done by a "a skilful
contrivance," since it played while held in his own
hands. This was done "in the open room, with the full
light upon it, [and] the regular action of the accordion
going on without any visible agency. . . ."

The greatest shocker in Bell's *Cornhill* story and the
part that caused the greatest furor was that dealing with
Home's floating in the air. Bell wrote:

Mr. Home was seated next to the window. Through the semi-darkness his head was dimly visible against the curtains. His hands might be seen in a faint white heap before him. Presently he said in a quiet voice, "My chair is moving—I am off the ground—don't notice me—talk of something else."

It was very difficult to restrain the curiosity, not un-mixed with a more serious feeling, which these few words awakened. But we talked, incoherently enough, upon some indifferent topic. I was sitting nearly oppo-site to Mr. Home. I saw his hands disappear from the table, and his head vanish into the deep shadow be-yond. In a moment or two more he spoke again. This time his voice was in the air above our heads. He had risen from his chair to a height of four or five feet from the ground.

As he ascended higher he described his position, as at first perpendicular, and afterwards horizontal. He said he felt as if he had been turned in the gentlest manner, as a child is turned in the arms of a nurse. In a moment or two, he told us that he was going to pass across the window, against the gray, silvery light of which he would be visible. We watched in profound stillness, and saw his figure pass from one side of the window to the other, feet foremost, lying horizontally in the air. He spoke to us as he passed. He told us that he would turn the reverse way, and recross the window; which he did. . . .

Home hovered round the circle for several minutes, and passed, this time perpendicularly, over our heads. I heard his voice behind me in the air, and felt something lightly brush my chair. It was his foot, which he gave me to touch. . . . He now passed over to the farthest extrem-ity of the room. We could judge by his voice of the altitude and distance he had attained. He had reached the ceiling, upon which he made a slight mark, and soon afterwards descended and resumed his place at the ta-ble.

Bell claimed that the self-playing accordion continued to play music with a wild pathos while Home floated in the air. The accordion was in the opposite corner of the room. At no time was it near the floating medium.

Since the article was published anonymously, Thackeray as editor of the *Cornhill Magazine* caught the brunt of the flood of condemnation that followed publication of Bell's article. Both Robert Browning and Charles Dickens derided Thackeray for publishing the article. Thackeray replied to all his critics that if they had seen what he had seen, they would not be so quick to condemn without making their own investigation. The charge of deriding spiritualism without having any firsthand knowledge of it was particularly hurled at Dickens. The distinguished author of *Oliver Twist* flatly refused to attend any séance, although he was constantly urged to do so.

Since the article, "Stranger than Fiction" was published anonymously and none of the participants were identified, critics charged that it was fiction. A Mr. John Coleman in a letter to the *Morning Star* newspaper challenged any other person present at the séance to come forward and support the *Cornhill* story. He intimated that he did not expect anyone to do so.

Immediately Dr. James M. Gully, editor of the *London Medical and Surgical Journal,* accepted the challenge. He had been present at the séance with Bell, which was held at the home of Mrs. Thomas Milner Gibson. Mr. Thomas Milner Gibson, a prominent politician, hated spiritualism as strongly as his wife supported it. Dickens, who knew them both, liked Mrs. Gibson, but considered her slightly crazy because of her devotion to spiritualism. Gully wrote:

I was one of the persons present at the evening meeting. The other gentlemen were a solicitor in extensive practice [Rymer?], and two writers of solid instructive works [Bell and Robert Chambers, an encyclopaedist. Gully's letter ignored the women present.]. . . . We were all workers in callings in which matters of fact, and not of fancy, especially come under observation. Further, it may be useful to some persons to know that we were neither asleep, nor intoxicated, nor even excited. We were complete masters of our senses. I submit that our evidence is worth a thousand conjectures and explanations by those who were not present.

I will state with the greatest positiveness that the record made in the article, *Stranger than Fiction*, is, in every particular, correct . . . and moreover, that no trick, machinery, sleight-of-hand, or other artistic contrivance produced what we saw and heard. . . .

Is it probable, is it possible, that any machinery could be . . . set up and previously made ready in a room which was fixed upon as a place of meeting only five minutes before we entered it? Could it be made capable of carrying such a weight [Home weighed between 140 and 154 pounds] about without the slightest sound of any description? . . .

Let it be remembered, moreover, that the room was, for a good part of the evening, in a blaze of light, in which no . . . machine sufficient for the purpose could be introduced; or, if already introduced, could remain unobserved. Even when the room was comparatively darkened, light streamed through the window from a distant gas-lamp outside. Between this gas-lamp and our eyes Mr. Home's form passed, so that we distinctly perceived its trunk and limbs.

Dr. Gully also added some things that were not in the *Cornhill* article. One of these involved Dr. Robert Chambers, who was identified in Gully's letter only as a "distinguished *littérateur*." According to Gully, Chambers' dead father was among the spirits who appeared that night. Chambers asked the spirit to prove itself by playing his father's favorite song.

> Addressing us, [Chambers] added, "The accordion was not invented at the time of my father's death. So I cannot conceive how he can play it."
>
> Almost immediately the flute notes of the accordion (which was upon the floor) played through *Ye Banks and Braes of Bonnie Doon*, which the gentleman [Chambers] assured us was his father's favorite air, whilst the flute was his father's favorite instrument.

Dr. Gully and Robert Bell were only two of many who left accounts of Daniel Home's levitations. Sir William Crookes, the noted scientist who later made exhaustive tests of Home's manifestations, said:

> The best cases of Home's levitation I witnessed were in my own house. On one occasion he went to a clear part of the room. After standing quietly for a minute, he told us he was rising. I saw him slowly rise up with a continuous gliding movement and remain about six inches off the ground for several seconds, when he slowly descended. On this occasion no one moved from their places. On another occasion I was invited to come to him, when he rose 18 inches off the ground. I passed my hands under his feet, round him, and over his head when he was in the air.
>
> On several occasions Home and the chair on which he was sitting at the table rose in the air. This was generally done very deliberately. Home sometimes then tucked up his feet on the seat of the chair, and held up his hands in view of all of us. On such an occasion I have got down and seen and felt that all four legs were off the ground at the same time, Home's feet being on the chair. Less frequently the levitating power extended to those sitting

next to him. Once my wife was thus raised off the
ground in her chair.

Daniel recounted in his memoirs an example of his
levitation. This occurred during a visit with the Count
and Countess de Beaumont at Bordeaux, France:

> The lady of the house turned to me and said abruptly,
> "Why you are sitting in the air!" On looking we found
> that the chair remained in its place, but that I was ele-
> vated two or three inches above it. My feet were not
> touching the floor. This may show how unconscious I
> am at times to the sensation of levitation.
>
> I was now impressed to leave the table and was soon
> carried to the lofty ceiling. The Count de B—— [Beau-
> mont] left his place at the table, and coming under where
> I was, said, "Now, young Home, come and let me touch
> your feet."
>
> I told him I had no volition in the matter, but perhaps
> the spirits would kindly allow me to come down to him.
> They did so, by floating me down to him. My feet were
> soon in his outstretched hands. He seized my boots, and
> now I was again elevated, he holding tightly, and pull-
> ing on my feet until the boots I wore, which had elastic
> sides, came off, and remained in his hands.

James Wason, a lawyer from Liverpool, England, attended a London séance of Home's, and left his account
of the medium's levitation:

> The curtains at last were drawn by invisible means, and
> then Mr. Home stated he was being lifted up in the air.
> He crossed the table over the heads of the parties sitting
> around it. I asked him to make a mark with his pencil on
> the ceiling. He said he had no pencil. I rose up and said I
> would lend him mine. By standing and stretching up-
> wards I was enabled to reach his hand, about seven feet
> distant from the floor. I placed therein a pencil. Keeping

hold of his hand, I moved along with him five or six paces as he floated above me in the air. I only let go of his hand when I stumbled against a stool.

Mr. Home, as he floated along, kept ringing the small hand-bell to indicate his locality in the room, which was probably thirty by forty feet.

The room was in total darkness. Despite continued claims that Home always worked in the light, he seems to have preferred a dark room for his levitation acts. However Mr. Wason claims he saw Home's body cross two beams of light shining through a crack in the door from the adjoining room, which was brightly lighted. These are but a few examples of many stories told about Home's levitation. The most remarkable of all the stories is the one mentioned in Chapter 1, when Home reputedly floated out a window and into another window for Lord Lindsay and his guests.

Did he really float around the room? Some of those who believed that Home did communicate with spirits also thought that he sometimes embellished his act with trickery to add to the effect. Floating mediums were not uncommon. Some of their methods have been exposed. Since Home worked in the dark during his levitation, this part of his repertoire must be viewed with a very critical eye. He seems to have picked up his ability to produce spirit rapping by himself. Apparently he had no contact with any known person who could have taught him. However, his levitation is something else. There is a direct line between him and another noted floater who could very well have passed along his secrets to Home, who was eighteen when they met. Levitation will be discussed more fully in Chapter 13.

Another of Home's performances that smacks of trickery was his handling of fire and burning coals. Fire

walking and magical handling of fire are among the
oldest tricks of esoteric magic. It was widely known
among scattered primitive tribes and survives to this
day.

This is not to say that Home's fire handling was a
fraud, but he is certainly open to suspicion.

Alfred Russel Wallace, the noted biologist, wrote in
his book, *Miracles and Modern Spiritualism:*

> Perhaps the best attested and most extraordinary
> phenomenon connected with Mr. Home's mediumship
> was what is called the fire-test. In a state of trance Home
> took a glowing coal from the hottest part of a bright fire,
> and carried it round the room, so that every one might
> see and feel that it was a real one.

Among those who witnessed this act were H. D.
Jencken, a lawyer who later married pioneer spiritualist
Katie Fox, Lord Lindsay and Lord Adare, and Mr. and
Mrs. S. C. Hall. Mrs. Hall wrote an account of the fire
handling in a letter to the Earl of Dunraven, father of
Lord Adare. It was later published in *The Spiritualist*
magazine. After telling how Home picked up a glowing
coal from the fireplace, Mrs. Hall wrote:

> Mr. Hall was seated nearly opposite to where I sat. I saw
> Mr. Home . . . deliberately place the lump of burning
> coal on his [Hall's] head. I have often wondered that I
> was not frightened, but I was not. I had perfect faith that
> [my husband] would not be injured.
>
> Someone said, "Is it not hot?" Mr. Hall answered,
> "Warm, but not hot." Mr. Home had moved a little way,
> but returned, still in a trance. He smiled, and seemed
> quite pleased, and then proceeded to draw up Mr. Hall's
> white hair over the red coal. Mr. Home drew the hair
> into a sort of pyramid, the coal, still hot, showing be-
> neath the hair.

Wallace claimed that after the coal was taken from Hall's head, where it did no damage, others who tried to touch it were burned. Wallace also reports that a man in Glasgow, Scotland, claimed to have seen Home place a live coal in a woman's hand. It did not burn her, but when removed and placed on a newspaper it caused a blaze.

Sir William Crookes also gave his version of the Home fire tests. In an address to the Society for Psychical Research, which was later printed in the society's journal, Crookes said:

> I several times saw the fire test, both at my own and at other houses. On one occasion Home called me to him when he went to the fire. He told me to watch carefully. He certainly put his hand in the grate and handled the red-hot coals in a manner which would have been impossible for me to have imitated without being severely burned. I once saw him go straight to a bright wood fire, and, taking a large piece of red-hot charcoal, put it in the hollow of one hand, and covering it with the other hand, blow into the extempore furnace until the coal was white hot and the flames licked around his fingers. No sign of burning could be seen then or afterwards on his hands.

In a later séance Crookes again saw Home handling fire. In a letter describing the strange event, Crookes wrote in 1871:

> I went with Home to the fireplace in the back drawing-room. He said, "We want you to notice particularly what Dan is doing." [When in a trance during a séance, Home often spoke of himself in the third person, as if a spirit voice were speaking through him.]
> Accordingly I stood close to the fire and stooped down to it when he put his hands in. Home very deliberately pulled the lumps of hot coal off, one at a time, with his

right hand and touched one which was bright red. He then said, "The power is not strong on Dan's hand, as we have been influencing the handkerchief most. It is more difficult to influence an inanimate body like that than living flesh. So, as the circumstances were favorable, we thought we would show you that we could prevent a red-hot coal from burning a handkerchief. We will collect more power on the handkerchief and repeat it for you now!"

Mr. Home then waved the handkerchief about in the air two or three times, held it up above his head and then folded it up and laid it on his hand like a cushion. He put his other hand into the fire, took out a large lump of cinder red-hot at the lower part and placed the red part on the handkerchief. Under ordinary circumstances it would have been in a blaze.

In about a half minute, Home took it off the handkerchief with his hand, saying, "As the power is not strong, if we leave the coal longer it will burn." He then put it on his hand and brought the coal to the table in the front room, where all but myself had remained seated.

At a different time, the Reverend W. Stainton Moses, an ardent spiritualist, recorded the following in his private notebooks of psychic occurrences:

Home then went to the fireplace, removed the guard, and sat down on the hearth rug. Then he seemed to hold a conversation by signs with a spirit. He repeatedly bowed, and finally set to work to mesmerize his head again. He ruffled his bushy hair until it stood out like a mop, and then deliberately lay down and put his head in the bright wood fire.

The hair was in the blaze, and must, under ordinary circumstances, have been singed off. Home's head was in the grate, and his neck was on a level with the top-bar. This was repeated several times. He also put his hand into the fire, smoothed away the wood and coal, and picked out a live coal which he held in his hand for a few seconds. He replaced it soon, saying the power was not sufficient.

Home tried to give a live coal to Mr. Crookes, but was unable to do it. He then came to all of us to satisfy us that there was no smell of fire in his hair. There was absolutely none.

Twenty years after this remarkable séance, a man named F. W. H. Myers wrote Sir William Crookes, inquiring as to the truth of Stainton Moses' account of the fire test. Crookes replied in a letter written on March 9, 1893. "I have a distinct recollection of the séance . . . and can corroborate Mr. Stainton Moses' account. . . ."

After several triumphant months in England, Home took his family back to Paris. Here at a séance in a chateau, Home's spirits proved that they could be amusing as well as awesome. The family and guests were sitting in the dark, for the spirits asked that the lights be extinguished. The curtains were pulled back, however, so that moonlight illuminated the room. One of the guests asked for a glass of brandy. As he raised the glass, a spirit hand came out of the darkness and took it from him. Hand and glass disappeared under the table. The group laughed and Home observed, "Our unseen friends apparently do not believe in stimulants!"

A chorus of raps told them that this was true. Then the glass floated up from under the table. It was empty. Several of the guests got down on the floor to see if the liquor had been emptied there. They found no wet spots. When they got back to their chairs, the glass moved without anything seeming to touch it to the edge of the table. It disappeared and then reappeared filled again with brandy.

Home was developing into quite a showman. At this

point he reached the heights of personal happiness. He was internationally famous. He had an adoring wife and a young son of whom he was particularly proud. Money was no longer a worry, since his wife had a small fortune. Unfortunately, sadness and tragedy lay just ahead.

12

GOOD YEARS
AND BAD YEARS

Home's return to Paris and then to Russia was a great
triumph. He was again received by Napoleon III in
France and by Alexander II in Russia. There were plans
to revisit Queen Sophie of the Netherlands, but this was
called off for diplomatic reasons. The queen's session
with Home in 1858 caused such criticism in her country
that the séances were not repeated. Among Home's
souvenirs was a hand-written note from the queen,
which she had sent him along with a ring. The note said,
"I send you a grateful souvenir of our séances—Sophie."

The blight on Home's life was the decline of his wife's
health. The exact nature of her trouble was not recorded,
Home reporting only that it was an internal disorder. In
any event, she grew steadily worse and died on July 3,
1862, at the home of her sister, the Countess Luba
Koucheleff-Besborodka. She was twenty-two years old.

She had been told the previous year that she was
dying. She took the announcement calmly, for she was a
confirmed spiritualist. She sincerely believed that she

was not dying, but merely passing to a different plane of existence. She thought she would still be able to communicate with her husband and that he would eventually join her in the spirit world.

Mrs. William Howitt, wife of the author of *The History of the Supernatural*, observed Mrs. Home during her last days and remarked on her serenity. Mrs. Howitt also wrote:

> Frequently, during the last two months of Mrs. Home's illness, not only she, but all those about her, heard delicious strains of spirit music, sounding like a perfect harmony of vocal sounds. During the last month, also, words were distinctly heard. They were recognized as the chants for the dying used in the Russian Church.

Mrs. Home died on a Thursday. On the following Saturday, her three-year-old son awoke in the morning and said to his nurse, "I have seen mamma, and she is well. She is with God, and she told me that my Uncle Gregoire and my Aunt Luba are my godfather and godmother, and that they would be very good to me, and I must love them."

Mrs. S. C. Hall, wife of the man whose hair Home wrapped around the glowing coal, had her own memories of Sacha Home's ghost. She told of a séance held immediately after Mrs. Home's death. "There were only five persons present," she said. "Five who had known and loved Sacha!"

Before her death Sacha had embroidered a little lace cap for the elderly Mrs. Hall. Home brought this cap to the séance, along with a lock of the dead girl's hair, for which Mrs. Hall had asked him. He placed them upon the table.

"Sacha," Home said, "wishes to give them to you herself."

"Presently," Mrs. Hall wrote later, "my dress was pulled. I put my hand down. The cap was not only placed in it, but my fingers closed over it, *by her hand*. I could not be mistaken. I know that hand so well!"

The death of Sacha Home left Daniel in a difficult financial position. They had lived well on her income, plus the $1,200 a year he received from the inheritance left him earlier by a woman admirer. However, Sacha's property was in Russia, and immediately after her death, some of her relatives seized it. Home sued, but in the manner of lawsuits the world over, the case dragged through the courts. This left him without funds, but since it appeared that he would eventually win the case, he had no difficulty getting credit.

He fell back into his old manner of living, traveling and staying as houseguest where he could. He had for some time been working on his memoirs, but found difficulty in putting his thoughts on paper. After a few weeks in France, he returned to London to get a lawyer friend, William M. Wilkinson, to help him with the writing. The book was completed in late 1862. There was some difficulty finding a publisher, until Dr. Robert Chambers arranged for his own publishers, Longman, Green, to look at the manuscript. It was accepted and published in 1863 under the title *Incidents in My Life*.

The book was hailed as a work of genius by spiritualists, and damned as fraud and fantastic fiction by others. Sir David Brewster threatened to sue, and Robert Browning, asked if he had read the book, replied that he had no time to waste on trash.

The book was successful, and a second printing appeared the following year, with an added preface quoting Sir David Brewster's threats of libel over remarks made about his controversy with Home. The book known as *Incidents in My Life, Second Series*, is an entirely new book written some years later.

Home came in for more notoriety the following year when Robert Browning finally published his long narrative poem, "Mr. Sludge." All who read the poem knew at whom Browning was directing his venom. However, Home himself professed not to see the resemblance between himself and Browning's charlatan.

"No person even slightly acquainted with me could discover one point of resemblance," Home said. However, he did admit that the poem was an attack upon spiritualism. He added that the piece was an insult to the memory of Elizabeth Barrett Browning, who had died in 1861.

Browning also continued to denounce Home in letters to his friends. In late 1863, Home—for some unknown reason—decided to become a sculptor. He went to Rome to persuade William Wetmore Story, the famous American sculptor living there, to take him as a student. Story refused, but Browning heard differently. He immediately wrote a friend that if Story "chooses to take this dung-ball into his hand . . . he will get more and more smeared."

During this stay in Rome, in January 1864, the chief of police in Rome invited Home to move elsewhere. He pointed out that the Vatican had placed *Incidents in My Life* on its index of banned books. Home angrily refused. When the police questioned him as to his claim that he talked with spirits, raps broke out all around the interrogation room.

Home appealed to the British consul, but got no assistance. He gave up fighting and left Rome. When he arrived back in London, there was an uproar over the way he had been dismissed from Rome. The anti-

Catholic press demanded that Parliament do something about such treatment of a British subject. (Although he lived many years in the United States, Home never relinquished his British citizenship.) The papacy ruled Rome at that time, and Home's friends asked the British Foreign Office to lodge a formal complaint. This was turned down. The Foreign Office secretary, Lord Russell, had an opinion of Home only slightly better than that held by Robert Browning. He saw no reason for disturbing Great Britain's diplomatic relations with the Vatican because the Pope did not want a spiritualist practicing in his neighborhood.

Throughout his career up to that time Home had been careful to disassociate himself from other mediums. He refused to attend any of their séances publicly, although he sometimes went in secret, as he had done at the Cora Hatch appearance in New York. When the Davenport brothers, Ira and William, appeared in London in 1864, Home refused all invitations to meet them. The two brothers, unlike Home, had been inspired by the Hydesville knocking and the Fox sisters. They became well-known mediums in the United States. Unlike Home, who kept his amateur status to the last, the Davenports developed a stage act. They had a spirit cabinet, and they invited a member of the audience to get in the cabinet with them. Then they were all three securely tied by volunteers from the audience. The cabinet door was closed. Musical instruments left in the cabinet were played. Objects belonging to the invited member of the audience were thrown out of the cabinet through the open top. But when the cabinet door was opened, all three persons were disclosed still bound by their ropes.

The secret was simple enough. It was not spirits in the cabinet who played the music and did the pranks. The

Davenports were pioneer escape artists. Using methods later made famous by Houdini, they slipped in and out of their rope bonds.

John Nevil Maskelyne, later a famous stage magician, exposed their tricks. Home was asked to give his opinion of Maskelyne's exposé. He refused. He did admit that many spiritualists were frauds and even went so far as to tell how these frauds were done. He was then working on the second series of his memoirs, and promised that, when they were completed, he would write a book on spiritualist frauds.

John Henry Anderson, the Wizard of the North, was the most famous stage magician of this period. He was violently antispiritualist, and worked hard to expose fraudulent mediums. However, he never commented publicly on Home.

Throughout these years Home never accepted money for his séances. Consequently, he could never be accused of robbing the public, as many of the other mediums were. The very worst that he could be charged with was tricking his friends. The only time he was involved in anything that smacked of dishonor was the legal battle that became notorious as the Home–Lyon Affair.

In 1866 Home met Mrs. Jane Lyon, a rich widow who was about seventy-five years old. Mrs. Lyon was greatly interested in spiritualism and fancied herself as a medium of sorts. She had read Home's book, *Incidents in My Life*, and sought him out. Vulgar, illiterate, and in awe of the nobility, Mrs. Lyon was more interested in the famous people Home had met than in the spirits he claimed to talk with. She never tired of listening to him tell of the kings, queens, counts, and countesses he knew.

According to the second Mrs. Home in her book:

> She astounded Mr. Home with the declaration that she
> had taken a great fancy to him. She was determined to
> adopt him as her son, and settle a handsome fortune
> upon him. She was rich, she explained, was without
> children or relatives of her own, and her husband's
> relatives she detested. He would add her name of Lyon
> to his own. They would keep house together as mother
> and son. Thus two people would be made happy, he in
> becoming rich through her means, she in being intro-
> duced through him to the fashionable world.

Daniel thought she was joking, but she repeated her
offer several times, saying that she would settle £24,000
on him. Thus was roughly $120,000 at the exchange rates
of the time. Home consulted his friend, S. C. Hall, and
then talked to W. M. Wilkinson, the lawyer who helped
him write his memoirs. Both men talked to Mrs. Lyon.
She insisted on her seriousness, saying, "What is
twenty-four thousand pounds to me in comparison with
having a son that I can love, and who will be kind to
me?"

Mrs. Lyon then sent Home a draft for the money,
accompanied by a letter that sounds as if it had been
dictated by a lawyer to cover Home in case he was later
charged—as a number of mediums had been—with taking advantage of foolish old women. The letter read:

> My dear Mr. Home,—I have a desire to render you inde-
> pendent of the world, and having ample means for the
> purpose without abstracting from any needs or comforts
> of my own, I have the greatest satisfaction in now
> presenting you with and as an entirely free gift from me
> the sum of £24,000, and am, my dear sir, yours very truly
> and respectfully, JANE LYON.

Home, on the advice of Wilkinson and Hall, accepted the offer. He then changed his name to Home-Lyon. Shortly after this, Mrs. Lyon went to Wilkinson and said she wanted to change her will, leaving all her fortune to Home. In the court case that came later, Wilkinson made a sworn statement that he tried to talk her out of this. At the same time, he said that he would not draw up the will because he was a friend of Home's. Mrs. Lyon insisted, and he went ahead.

A short time later she informed Wilkinson that she wanted to give Home an additional £6,000. She said she intended to transfer most of her property to Home while she still lived in order to escape inheritance taxes on the property when she died. Wilkinson's statement in court claimed:

> I again warned her against being in any way influenced by any spirit-communication, or by anything but her own unbiased opinion. She assured me she was not. . . . She said that whatever happened, she had more money than she could want. She was only too glad to make Daniel independent after all he had suffered.

Mrs. Lyon was still not through. She executed a trust-deed transferring an additional £30,000 to Home. Soon after this, their relationship began to turn bad. Home became seriously ill, which made Mrs. Lyon complain that she was tied to a dying man. She hated children and took a violent dislike to Home's young son. She ordered Home never to bring the child near her again. She decided to change her will for fear Home would die and that "detestable child" would get her money. The second Mrs. Home, in her book, claims that Mrs. Lyon was even more disappointed in her social reception. She had expected her adopted son to gain her an entrance into high society.

> She was grievously disappointed with her reception in society where Home moved, and to which he had introduced her. His friends saw as little as possible of her; for she was as ignorant of the ways and habits of well-bred people, as destitute of their breeding. With this disappointment working on her violent temper . . . she determined to recall a portion at least of her gifts. In May, 1867, she consulted a retired barrister.

Home had been at Malvern taking treatments from Dr. Gully. He returned to London in June and went to see his foster mother. Mrs. Lyon demanded "in language of outrageous abuse and insult, the return of the trust-deed giving Home the second £30,000." Among other things, Mrs. Lyon accused Home and his friends, Hall and Wilkinson, of persuading her to give the money to Home against her better judgment.

Daniel, keeping his temper, replied that he would return the last gift of £30,000 if Mrs. Lyon would give him a written statement retracting the charges she made against him and his friends. She replied by filing charges against Home. He was arrested on June 18, 1867, but was released when he deposited the remainder of the entire £60,000. Part of the money had been spent in living expenses. He had also sent money to buy a house for his aunt, Mary Cook, in the United States.

The case was not tried until April 1868. The judge repeatedly accused Mrs. Lyon of lying. However, the court decision went against Home. The money was ordered returned to Mrs. Lyon, but she was ordered to pay all court costs both for herself and for Home.

The lawsuit did not hurt Home in the eyes of his close friends, but the general public, through newspaper coverage of the trial, got the impression that here was another fraudulent medium using his ghost friends to prey upon a foolish woman.

Robert Browning was delighted. He was gleeful because Home was being tried for "getting money under false pretences." He claimed that Hall and Wilkinson were in league with Home to fleece Mrs. Lyon, saying the two "got pretty pickings out of the plunder." Browning went on to say that the case turned on the testimony of a devoted servant of Mrs. Lyon, who had listened at the door. The servant testified that Home had indeed told Mrs. Lyon that the spirit of her dead husband advised her to give Home money. Home denied this vigorously.

This was the darkest blot on Home's entire career, and it left him bitter. He now wanted to withdraw from his séances, but could not do so immediately. The lawsuit over his wife's Russian estate was not yet settled. The loss of the Lyon money was a financial blow. Invitations to be a houseguest were not coming as frequently as they once did. So, for the first time in his life, Home had to go to work. However, he still refused to become a paid medium. Instead he arranged to tour England and Scotland to give literary readings. Charles Dickens had done quite well at this, reading his own works. Now the man Dickens hated followed his lead, but used the weird works of Edgar Allan Poe. Critics agreed that Home did a splendid job, and the tour was an enormous success. At the same time, it also brought him back into fashion as a performing guest. Everywhere he went Home was deluged with invitations, many of which he accepted.

His next job was the unlikely one of war correspondent. His friend Lord Adare arranged it. Adare had been a correspondent in the British-Abyssinian War. So when the Prussian states and France went to war in 1870, Adare found positions for both himself and Home. Strangely, considering his great friendship with Napoleon III and Empress Eugénie, Home was accredited to the German army. He did a passable job as a writer, but spent much time with séances for high-ranking officers of the army.

After the fall of France, Home went to Russia, where he received a royal welcome from his old friends. At a reception one evening Home saw a tall, regal, and lovely woman, Julie de Gloumeline. She was the sister-in-law of the distinguished professor of chemistry at St. Petersburg, Alexander von Boutlerow. Here is how the heiress described her meeting with Home:

> I first saw Mr. Home in February, 1871. I expected to find a personage occupied with his own celebrity. I was agreeably surprised to meet, on the contrary, a man in whom there was no trace of pretension. A smile of seductive good-humor, reflected a winning nature, and gave a marked charm to his expressive features. His form and bearing denoted race. His affable disposition indicated that Scottish nationality of which he was justly proud. . . . At the moment of his being presented to me . . . I heard only a voice saying to me, "Here is your husband." Home at the same instant received the same impression. It was so real, so instantaneous, that it did not even come to me with a feeling of surprise. A mutual accord was established at once between us.

When Home left Russia, he and Julie were engaged. It was understood that the wedding would be in Paris in the fall. From Russia he went directly to London, where he began his famous work with Sir William Crookes. Crookes, one of the notable scientists of his day, believed in spiritualism and was determined to prove it scientifically.

13

SCIENCE
VERSUS FRAUD
AND SUPERSTITION

William Crookes was an outstanding chemist and physicist. He discovered the element thallium and invented the Crookes tube, which produced cathode rays. The Crookes tube led to the development by others of X rays and the cathode tube used in television. He edited two science magazines and was involved in a number of important inventions. He was so noted for his scientific approach that, when he announced that he would investigate spiritualism, one paper said, "At last we will get to the bottom of this thing."

Crookes first met Home in 1869, but did not begin his famous series of experiments with the Scots medium until 1871. The previous year Crookes attended several Home séances, but had done no more than look under the table and search for tricks. Now he intended to give a full scientific investigation.

One of the things Crookes especially investigated was the self-playing accordion. The most obvious explanation is that there was a hidden clockwork music box inside. However Crookes, in his report published in the *Quarterly Journal of Science* for July 1, 1871, says that they did not use Home's accordion: "The accordion was a new one, having been purchased by myself for the purpose of these experiments. Mr. Home had neither handled nor seen the instrument before the commencement of the test experiments."

Crookes also wanted to assure himself that no outside agency was pulling on the instrument with wires or threads. He made a wooden frame and bound it with twenty-four turns of copper wire to make a wire cage. These horizontal strands of wire—wound an inch apart—were then joined with string to make a tight mesh. He also arranged two batteries so they could be connected to the copper wire.

There were eight persons present, including Crookes and Home. One was a scientist, another was a lawyer. Crookes's wife, his brother and his wife, and Crookes's laboratory assistant were also witnesses. Crookes said:

Mr. Home sat in a low easy chair at the side of the table. In front of him under the table was the test cage. One of his legs was on each side of it. I sat close to him on his left. Another observer sat close to him on his right. The rest of the party were seated at convenient distances round the table.

For the greater part of the evening, particularly when anything of importance was proceeding, the observers on each side of Mr. Home kept their feet respectively on his feet, so as to be able to detect his slightest movement.

The temperature of the room varied from 68° to 70° F.

Mr. Home kept the accordion between the thumb and middle finger of one hand at the opposite end to the keys.

Crookes said that the wire cage was pulled from under the table just enough for Home to get the accordion and his hand into it. It was then pushed back under the table "as close as Mr. Home's arm would permit, but without hiding his hand from those next to him."

A woodcut shows Home with the wire cage William Crookes put around the accordion to prove that no outside agency was involved in playing it.

Very soon the accordion was seen by those on each side to be waving about in a somewhat curious manner. Then sounds came from it, and finally several notes were played in succession. Whilst this was going on, my assistant went under the table. He reported that the accordion was expanding and contracting. At the same time it was seen that the hand of Mr. Home [by which the accordion was held] was quite still. His other hand rested on the table.

Presently the accordion was seen by those on either side of Mr. Home to move about, oscillating and going round and round the cage, playing at the same time. . . .

We heard distinct and separate notes sounded in succession, and then a simple air was played. As such a result could only have been produced by the various keys of the instrument being acted upon in harmonious succession, this was considered by those present to be a crucial experiment.

But the sequel was still more striking. Mr. Home removed his hand altogether from the accordion, taking it quite out of the cage, and placed the accordion in the hand of the person next to him. [This was either Crookes himself or Mrs. Crookes.] The instrument then continued to play, *no person touching it and no hand being near it.*

There had been attempts to explain spiritualist manifestations in terms of electromagnetic and other natural forces. In other words, a certain person might have a greater concentration of psychic force in his body than others. This would permit him to do things others could not, and this would appear to be supernatural, when actually it was natural enough.

In an attempt to check this, Crookes wound twenty-four turns of copper wire around his accordion cage. After the first experiments, Crookes then connected this wire coil to batteries. He hoped that the electrical current flowing through the wire would serve to block, distort, or increase any true psychic force that might be operating the accordion.

The current had no effect whatsoever.

Crookes also rigged up a board and a balance scale in an attempt to prove or disprove that Home possessed a psychic force that could act independent of his conscious muscle movement. The test called for Home to put his fingers lightly on the opposite end of the board. Any force this exerted would show on the scales. The board weighed three pounds. When Home touched it, the scale moved up to 6½ pounds.

Crookes watched Home closely to make sure the medium only lightly touched his fingertips to the board. Then Crookes himself pressed on the end of the board with all his strength. The scales indicator moved only 1½ pounds. This convinced Crookes that there was no way that Home could have moved the scales so much unless aided by psychic force.

Despite his fame as a scientist, Crookes's announcement of experiments that tended to prove a new type of force previously unknown to physics brought down on him the accumulated wrath of his scientific colleagues.

At the conclusion of this series of tests, Home left Crookes to argue with his fellow scientists and returned to Europe. In Paris, he and Julie de Gloumeline were married in a brilliant ceremony in the Russian Orthodox Church. The couple then went to Russia for their honeymoon, where the czar presented the couple with a beautiful sapphire-diamond ring. Finally, in the spring of 1872, the slow-moving Russian courts decided in Daniel's favor in the lawsuit over his former wife's property. His new wife was also wealthy. At last Home was financially independent.

He announced that he would give no more séances. However, he did agree to complete his tests with William Crookes. The scientist's records show that these resumed in April 1872. Seven séances were held before they ended in July 1873.

One held in 1872 was notable for bringing together Katie Fox and Daniel Home. It was Katie's questions to the Hydesville rapper that began modern spiritualism. Except for Daniel's 1872 visit with Henry Gordon in Springfield, Massachusetts, this was the only medium Home ever worked with.

Twenty-four years had passed since Katie and her sister Margaretta began to talk with ghosts. They had been bitter years for both of them. Their older sister, Leah Fox Underhill, was the driving force behind them. Ambitious, hungry for money, Leah several times prevented the girls from quitting spiritualism.

The girls had a harder time than Home. They had been cursed, reviled, and insulted by groups who accused them of being in league with the devil. Once a mob stormed the hall where they were holding a séance, and they had to be rescued by the police. They were constantly accused of fraud. This was mainly because of their public séances, whereas Home performed only for wealthy friends in the privacy of their homes.

Unhappiness with her public life had turned Katie Fox into an alcoholic. She was then about thirty-six years old. Her age at the time of the Hydesville rappings was given by her mother, at different times, as ranging from eight to fourteen. Most authorities believe she was born in 1833. This would have made her fifteen at the time of the first rappings. It appears more likely that she was eleven or twelve.

Katie Fox as she appeared during her trip to England in 1871.

She still had an enormous reputation as a medium, and the London spiritualist circles came out in force to do her honor. Some years before she had been exposed as a fraud by a woman named Ruth Culver. Mrs. Culver was a relative of the wife of the Fox sisters' brother David.

Mrs. Culver made her statement against the sisters at the urging of C. Chauncy Burr, a man whom Leah Fox Underhill was suing for libel after he claimed the rappings were made by snapping the girls' toe joints. "Toe-ology," he called it. It was published in the New York *Express*. Mrs. Culver claimed she had originally believed in the rappings, but closer observation of Katie and Margaretta convinced her that the girls were frauds.

Margaretta was absent. Mrs. Culver worked to gain Katie's confidence and suggested that she would like to help. "After I had helped her a few times, she revealed to me the secret. The raps are produced with the toes. All the toes are used. After nearly a week's practice, with Katharine helping me, I could produce them perfectly myself. . . . She also told me all I had to do to make the raps heard on the table would be to put my foot against the bottom of the table when I rapped. When I wished to make the raps sound distant on the wall, I must make them louder, and direct my eyes to the spot where I wished them to be heard."

The exposé backfired on Burr. It did not hurt the Fox sisters at all. Though some newspapers thundered at the fraud, spiritualists refused to believe it. Home, when asked if the raps could be made by cracking the joints of one's toes, laughed uproariously. The story was also told to Crookes before he began his tests with Katie. He said such a thing was impossible.

Crookes said that Home's raps were more varied, "but for power and certainty I have met with no one who at all approached Miss Kate Fox."

Although William Crookes was a scientist and a sincere investigator, he was also a firm believer in spiritualism. He, while trying to be scientifically detached, wanted to find proof of his beliefs. In such a condition, it is easy for the most sincere investigator to be fooled. He is not then a good witness. Neither were most of the others who observed the Crookes tests.

Fortunately there was one nonspiritualist present at some of the séances involving both Daniel Home and Katie Fox. He was Napier Broome, a reporter for the

London *Times*. Broome wrote a long story. The *Times* editors, mindful of the rash of condemnation that came anytime a publication supported spiritualism, held the story for some time before getting the courage to run it. Even then some of the material Broome included about Home's levitation and fire handling was omitted.

The Broome story, published without by-line, appeared in the issue of Thursday, December 26, 1872:

Our fourth and last séance occurred at a private house. There were nine persons present, including Mr. D. Home and Miss Fox, the well-known American medium. We formally searched the room and examined the furniture before we sat down at the table. . . .

The room was at first well-lighted from a gasburner overhead. On the table was an accordion, which we took to pieces and tried, and found to be in every respect an ordinary instrument. . . .

Almost immediately loud raps appeared from the table and the floor. Miss Fox then got up and went to the door of the room. She invited us to stand by her and to hold her hands, which we did. Loud thumps seemed to come from the panels as if done with a fist.

To give a detailed account of everything which occurred would need more space than we can now spare. Suffice it to say, that the table was made light and heavy at our wish. It moved in every direction. There were vibrations of the floor and of our chairs. Then Mr. Home, holding the accordion under the table in his right hand and by the end farthest from the keys, played a distinct tune. His left hand was on the table and his feet so raised as to be visible. All other hands were on the table.

At the same time, and under the same conditions, a small hand-bell was rung in different parts of the space beneath the table. The gas [light] was now turned out and two spirit lamps lit. These gave a fair light. The raps became louder. . . .

The reporter then says that he put his own hand under the séance table. The accordion floated into his hands. He held it in the same manner as Home had—by the end opposite the keys. The instrument continued to play a few bars. Then the hand-bell was pressed into his hand. He had difficulty holding both the bell and the accordion. Next a sprig of flowers was also thrust to him by, presumably, ghost hands.

At the end of the article Broome disclaimed any belief in spiritualism. This disclaimer is often omitted when spiritualist writers quote this famous article. Some have said that it did not reflect the writer's true opinion, but had been added because the *Times* editor insisted upon it. There is no proof of this, however.

> Yet even with all this, we are not a Spiritualist, and do not believe in a "Psychic Force." We remember and lay heart to Mr. G. H. Lewes's admirable maxim, "Distinguish between facts and inferences from facts." We are certain that the table rose from the ground, that our hand received a sprig from under the table from what felt like another hand. How these things happened we do not know. The nature of the phenomena and of human nature are such as to force us to suspect imposture and legerdemain until we can satisfy ourselves of the true causes, whatever these may be.

After the conclusion of the Crookes tests, Home definitely retired as a medium. In 1872 he published the second series of his memoirs and then wrote an exposé of spiritualism called *Light and Shadows of Spiritualism*. In this revealing book he told how fake spiritualists deluded and defrauded gullible people. When Home revealed that he was writing this book, he received threatening letters. He ignored them, and the book was finally published in 1877. At no time, however, did he cast any doubt upon his own work. He challenged the frauds to do as he did—work in the light and permit full examination of all he did.

Home condemned not only the fraudulent mediums themselves, but was even harder upon spiritualist societies made up of strong believers. Their hunger and demand for still greater miracles were what inspired the crooks, Home claimed.

For the rest of his life Home traveled restlessly from one place to another, unable to put down roots anywhere. Accompanied by his wife and son, he was pleasant to old friends, but refused to give séances. After the death of Napoleon III, the former Empress Eugénie sent Home frantic messages begging him to see her. She did not give the reason for her desire to see him, but Home knew that she wanted him to bring her into contact with the dead emperor. Home ignored Eugénie's letters and turned down the emissaries she sent to persuade him.

He loved to talk about the years of his international triumph and always wore part of the enormous collection of jewels given him by the crowned heads of Europe. Upon being asked, he could recite the history of each piece, telling who had given it to him and the circumstances. And though he talked freely of his séances with lesser people, he never discussed what went on when he performed for a crowned head. Accounts of these have come down in the memoirs of less reticent people who were there.

Home's health grew increasingly bad, until he died of tuberculosis at Auteuil, France, on June 21, 1886. He was fifty-three years old. At his request he was buried beside his daughter (by his second wife) who died in early infancy. Julie Home then returned to Russia with Home's son by his first marriage. Mrs. Home, however, worked hard to keep her husband's memory green. She wrote two books: *The Life and Mission of D. D. Home* and *The Gift of D. D. Home.*

14

WAS HOME A FRAUD?

Could Daniel Home actually converse with spirits? Or was he a cynical fraud playing on the credulity of the famous people for whom he performed?

One by one the major mediums of his day were exposed as frauds, swindlers, and crooks. The Fox sisters were exposed several times and finally—years after Home's death—Margaretta Fox, with Kate sitting beside her, acknowledged that they were frauds. Later Margaretta recanted this confession.

Home, however, never was exposed. Robert Browning's claims that he caught Home were untrue. Home maintained to the end that his séances were legitimate. His claim was supported by some very famous people, but they were disputed by others equally famous. Houdini, the most famous magician America ever produced, claimed he could duplicate through stagecraft anything Home did. John Nevil Maskelyne, Britain's most famous magician, said the same thing. John Mulholland, another famous American magician, also claimed that all Home's manifestations could be reproduced by trickery, but Mulholland—more honest than many of Home's critics—added, "It was never proven that he used the methods he could have used."

Mulholland's statement is very important in assessing Daniel Home. As any magician knows—or should know—there are more ways than one to do any trick. Home never revealed how he did his tricks, if indeed they were tricks, and therefore no one can say with certainty how they were done.

Floating above the audience was demonstrated by the British magician John Nevil Maskelyne during an exposé of spiritualism in London. The Davenport brothers' spirit cabinet, also exposed, is shown in the background.

It is true that any kind of trick can be produced on the magicians' stage. At Egyptian Hall in London, John Nevil Maskelyne floated in the air, rising from the stage and floating over the heads of his audience. Maskelyne used a carefully made dummy filled with hydrogen gas.

The face was a lifelike wax mask. There is a story that the head was made for Maskelyne by the marvelous technicians who worked for Madame Tussaud's famous waxworks museum in London.

This has been used as an example of how Home could have done his floating séances. Sir William Crookes blasted this theory. He pointed out that Home did not operate on a remote stage removed from his audience. He worked in the rooms of houses—many of which he had never visited before. It was impossible for him to have introduced gas-filled dummies. It was even more impossible to use gas-filled balloons to lift him in an ordinary room of a house. A gas balloon large enough to lift a 140-pound man could not have been concealed.

Then how did Home float himself? His secret went to the grave with him. However, there is a method that was used by some fraudulent mediums. One nineteenth-century exposé of mediums had a woodcut showing the trick in operation. It can only be done in darkness. The medium begins talking (as Home sometimes did):

"I am rising in the air! I am one foot off the floor! I am rising higher! I am now floating horizontally in the air!"

No one can see anything. They have only the wizard's word. But then the awed audience suddenly has proof! The floating man moves slowly toward one of the audience. The rest can hear his voice move across the room. The medium invites the man he approaches to reach out and touch his feet. The man does so and touches the upturned shoes of the medium floating five or six feet off the floor. The man naturally cries out for the benefit of the others that the medium *is* floating in the air, for he has touched the floating man.

Consider the statement of lawyer James Wason (see chapter 11): "Home *stated* he was being lifted up in the air. I moved along with him five or six paces as he floated above me in the air. I only let go of his hand when I stumbled against a stool."

The room was in total darkness, but Wason does say that there were two shafts of light coming from cracks in the door. He claims he saw Home's body pass across them. However, the entire story sounds much like that of the exposed medium who placed his shoes on his hands and invited the audience to feel them in the dark.

The story of how Home floated out the window at Lord Lindsay's house and back in a second window is much harder to explain. The windows were on the third story of the house. Houdini, in London in 1922, claimed that he could duplicate the trick. Spiritualists declared they would not be satisfied with a stage performance. It would be necessary for Houdini to perform the levitation act under the *exact conditions and in the exact location* Home did.

It must be remembered that Home had never been in Lord Lindsay's home before. Not until he walked into the room did he know which chamber in the house Lindsay had chosen for the séance. Often Home was searched before an exhibition to prove that he had no apparatus concealed upon his body.

The Houdini exhibition did not come off. The great magician explained that some difficulty had occurred with his assistant. He promised, however, to make the exhibition the next time he was in London. He never did.

Naturally, spiritualists smiled knowingly at Houdini's backdown. He had admitted that he needed an assistant. Home never had one. He never revealed his secrets even to his wives. If he had had a secret assistant, it would have been impossible to keep the secret from coming out. It would have been even more impossible to have introduced him into exclusive royal circles. It was also suggested that he bribed the servants, but in some of his most spectacular séances he never left the presence of witnesses from the time of his arrival to the séance.

Home began his spiritualist career as a table rapper and clairvoyant. He was then a teenage boy, who apparently had no contact with any other medium. Spirit rapping he learned himself. But in 1852—when Daniel was nineteen—he went to Massachusetts and met Henry Gordon, a well-known medium. Home said only that he met Gordon and was invited to attend a séance where very little happened. He then intimated that he left Gordon to visit the Rufus Elmer family. However, Emma Hardinge, the flamboyant spiritualist believer who wrote *Modern American Spiritualism*, knew Gordon well. She leaves the impression that Home worked with Gordon for much longer than Home claimed. Thus Gordon could well have been Home's teacher. She definitely states that they were practicing the floating-body manifestations at that time:

> In Springfield and Boston, Massachusetts, D. D. Home—afterwards renowned for his extraordinary mediumistic gifts throughout the courts of Europe— Henry C. Gordon, George Redman, and Rollin Square, were all developed for physical manifestations of the most wonderful kind.
>
> These young men were frequently lifted up in the air and floated over several feet of ground in the presence of hundreds of witnesses.

Miss Hardinge also quotes from the New York *Express* a story that said, "Mr. Henry Gordon, a well-known medium for spiritual manifestations, being at a circle in this city . . . was repeatedly raised from his seat and carried through the room, without any visible hand touching him. . . ."

Gordon was making these levitations not only at the time Home visited him, but had been doing them for two years previous.

Home was constantly accused of fraud, and many explanations were given in his lifetime as to how his "manifestations" were done. He noted some of them in one of his books:

> Some instances of the manner in which it is said the phenomena are produced are sufficiently amusing to be repeated. A very popular idea in Paris was that I carried in my pocket a tame monkey trained to assist me.
>
> Another is that my legs are so formed as to be capable of elongation, and that my feet are like those of a baboon. Many people suppose that when I go to a strange house, my tables have to be sent first, and that . . . they are always copiously draped. And that I take with me wax hands and arms to show at the proper moment.
>
> Some suppose that I magnetize or biologize [hyp-notize?] my audience, and that [the audience] only imag-ines they see what they see. Some think I carry with me lazy tongs and a magic lantern. Others have stated that when I am said to rise in the air, it is only a balloon filled with gas in the shape of a man. Others again will have it that [the levitation] is done by a magic lantern, whilst some doctors declare that I administer a thimbleful of chloroform to each of the sitters. . . .
>
> Some have enough spiritual belief to say that I have the devil at command. Others that I raise spirits by forms and incantations. . . .

We might say here that though some ignorant people did accuse Home of black magic, practitioners of this form of occult art did not accept Home as one of themselves. At this time black magic had quite a following in both London and Paris. The reason they did not accept Home is because black magic deals with evil, and its spirits are devilish and malignant. They are forced to appear through the power of the black magicians' spells and incantations and rituals. On the other hand, spiritualism's spirits are benign. These spirits dwell, in the view of spiritualists, in a happy land and communicate through mediums attuned to their world because of their regard for those left behind. They are not to be feared like the ghastly demonic spirits of black magic.

Continuing Home's account of the different ways he supposedly achieves his effects:

> Dr. Carpenter accounts for the phenomena as being produced by unconscious cerebration [presumably by action of the subconscious mind]. Mr. Morell, the philosopher, tells us that they are caused by "the reflex action of the mind." A common explanation is ventriloquism. Electricity is another. It is said that I have an electric battery concealed about my person. Then there are the od [odic] force and fluid action, and the nervous principle, and collusion, illusion and delusion.
>
> Mechanical contrivances attached to the lower extremities are also suggested by Sir David Brewster, but without specifying their particular nature. But the most scientific and learned explanation, leaving no room for conjectures, was given by an old woman in America, who when asked if she could account for what she had seen, replied, "Lor, Sirs, it's easy enough. He only rubs himself all over with a gold pencil."
>
> The rappings are said to be produced in many ways, each philosopher having his own theory, beginning low down with the snappings of the toe-joints [as the Fox sisters were said to have done] others getting up to the ankle, whilst some maintain it to be the knees, or thigh bones. . . . It has even been attributed to a strong beat-

ing of my pulse. Some say I rub my boots together, others my finger nails, and that springs are concealed in the table and about the room.

It has been said that I have an electrical quality which I can throw off at the command of my will. A general belief is that I bribe the servants at whatever house I visit, that they may aid me in concealing my machinery. The intelligence displayed in obtaining names, dates, and other circumstances, is previously communicated to me either by my own inquiry from servants or by visiting the tombstones of the relatives, or even by a body of secret police who are in my pay.

Others know that I am clairvoyant, and that I read the thoughts of those present. I am an accomplished juggler according to others, and have always refused to be seen by others of the craft, although the fact is quite the contrary. The greatest juggler of France has stated that he could not at all account for what he witnessed by any of the principles of his art.

However flattering all this might be to my vanity, in conferring upon me such astounding qualities and scientific achievements which I do not possess, it has been to me a source chiefly of amusement and wonder. . . .

Some of these "solutions" to the Home mystery are ridiculous, but we would be foolish to dismiss them all as methods he may have used just because he laughs at them. Such misdirection is not unknown among frauds and stage magicians also. Once Dunninger, a major American stage magician and mentalist, was talking to a group of fellow magicians. He was smoking a cigarette. He took it from his mouth.

"You know how to vanish this?" he asked them.

They nodded, for it was a well-known trick.

"But have you ever seen it done *this* way?" Dunninger asked.

He vanished the burning cigarette, laughed and walked off, leaving his peers scratching their heads and trying to figure out what he had done.

Actually, he had done nothing new. He went through the old routine exactly, but since they were expecting something new, they looked for something new. The majority of spiritualists during this period desperately wanted to find a link between the dead and the living. They were not critical. They wanted to believe.

It would appear that men like Sir William Crookes, and later Sir Oliver Lodge and Sir Arthur Conan Doyle would not have been fooled. Unfortunately, they, like the rest, wanted to believe. Conan Doyle is a classic example. Here was a man who had studied medicine and had also written the Sherlock Holmes detective stories. Surely the creator of Sherlock Holmes could have detected fraud. Yet Conan Doyle was taken in by a fake "spirit photograph" so crude that even ardent spiritualists were embarrassed by Sir Arthur's claim that the picture showed invisible fairies.

Others, like Michael Faraday, Charles Wheatstone, and David Brewster fitted theories to their disbelief without actually investigating Home at all. Brewster was the only one of the three who witnessed a séance, and his investigation consisted only of looking under the table.

In his report on investigation of Home and other mediums, Crookes listed eight theories to account for spiritualistic phenomena:

1. *Trickery*. "The phenomena are all the result of tricks, clever mechanical arrangements, or legerdemain; the mediums are impostors and the rest of the company are fools."

2. *Delusions.* "The persons at a séance are victims of a sort of mania or delusion, and imagine phenomena to occur which has no real objective existence."

3. *Cerebral Action.* "The whole is a result of conscious or unconscious cerebral actions." It is not clear what Crookes means here. Cerebral actions in this case are defined as "conceived by the intellect rather than the emotions." This would thus appear to mean that the audience mentally convinces itself, which is really delusion. Or it could mean that the medium creates these things with his mind so strongly that the audience actually sees them.

4. *Benign Spirits.* "This is the results of the spirit of the medium working in association with the spirits of some or all of the people present to provide a force to penetrate the unseen."

5. *Evil Spirits.* "The actions of evil spirits or devils . . . in order to undermine Christianity and ruin men's souls."

6. *Other Dimensions.* "The actions of a separate order of beings, living on this earth, but invisible and immaterial to us. Able, however, to manifest their presence occasionally."

7. *Spirits of the Dead.* "The actions of departed human beings—the spiritual theory *par excellence.*"

8. *Psychic Force.* "The theory of Psychic Force is . . . the recognition that under certain conditions . . . the bodies of certain persons . . . a Force operates by which, without muscular contact or connection, action at a distance is caused. . . . [Spiritualists] assert that the Spirits of the Dead can only do the acts attributed to them by using the Magnetism [that is, the Psychic Force] of the Medium."

Many of the stories about the wonderful things Home

did are suspect, simply because those telling them were ardent spiritualists who *wanted* to believe. Consequently, let us take the story of the London *Times* reporter Broome and consider each mystic occurrence he records in the light of how it could have been faked.

He records mysterious rappings, a table that became light or heavy upon command, an accordion that played itself, a bell that rang under the table when there was no one close enough to touch it, and a sprig of flowers pushed into his hands by ghostly hands. Although not included in his story because of editorial objections, he also saw fire handling and levitation.

What follows does not purport to tell *what* happened, but is intended to give *one* way by which these phenomena *could* have been faked. We must at the same time, in fairness to the memory of Home, keep in mind what magician Mulholland said about there being no proof that Home used any such methods.

First the rapping. This has been explained by Mrs. Culver in her exposé of the Fox sisters. Margaretta Fox admitted that this exposé was true in her famous confession (later denied, of course). That is, the noise was made by snapping the joints of the toes. We are told that the noises came from all directions by many authors. However, one we can trust, Sir William Crookes, in his account of the dual séance of Daniel Home and Kate Fox said that Kate got up from the table and stood near the door, after which rappings were heard coming from the wall near her. Standing in such a position removed from the others, she had only to make her noises while turning her head to stare at the wall to direct the audience's attention to that spot. This is a basic principle of ventriloquism. I have personally seen demonstrations of groans coming from a wall that were done in this manner. The groans came from the throat of the medium, who did not move his lips. He turned his head and stared at the wall, directing our attention. The effect was very good.

Crookes has written that it is incorrect to call these noises "raps." He said they came in a variety of sounds; some like raps on wood, but others ranged from sounds like scratches to heavy hammering noises. This indicates that a variety of methods were used, as the occasion demanded.

The table that tipped and became light or heavy on command is a staple trick of fake mediums. Take a piece of flat steel, fasten it around your forearm with leather bands. Make sure that the end of the steel does not stick out beyond the end of your cuff so that it will not be seen. Then when you sit at the séance table, you place your fingertips on top of the table for all to see, but at the same time you slide your hand far enough inward that the steel bar is pushed under the edge of the table. Then an upward pressure of your arms will cause the steel bar to lift up the table.

We were told in one account that the table rose so high that Home had to stand up from his chair to keep his hands on *top* of the table. We can bet he did! With the table lifted in such a manner he could invite someone, as he often did, to take a lamp and look under it. This person would not see anything, for he would be looking for rods or apparatus pushing out of the floor.

This method was popular with fake mediums who did not use raps for communication with their spirits, but who had the table beat out the raps by lifting and bumping back against the floor.

Home might have used something like this in his experiments for Crookes when his "Psychic Force" was tested by touching a board attached to a spring scale.

The accordion that played itself is the hardest of all to explain—much harder, in fact, than the famous fire handling. The obvious explanation is that he had a specially prepared instrument with a clockwork music box hidden inside. Clockwise-animated figures and apparatus were very popular in the eighteen and nineteenth centuries. The British magician Pinchbeck and the French conjurer Robert-Houdin were both famous for the automata they built. P. T. Barnum, the great showman, told in his autobiography of buying a picture-drawing automata from Robert-Houdin. So it would have been no trick for a skilled technician to make a self-playing accordion or guitar.

We are told by too many people to doubt it that Home arrived for his séances in strange houses accompanied by friends. He carried nothing in his hands. He was often searched. Of course, we have the story of Brewster that Home left the table during their séance. Brewster claimed it was to pick up apparatus (possibly the steel table raiser). Home claimed he was coughing blood and went for a handkerchief. He may have done so, but when we are investigating spiritualist phenomena, we must be suspicious of every movement.

In the case of the self-playing accordion, Crookes tells in one account that he bought a new instrument for the séance. Home had never seen it before. Broome says they tore the accordion apart before the séance to prove that there was nothing inside.

This leaves us with three possible explanations, since this was before there was any method of recording sound. One is that Home found some way to switch accordions, which is unlikely. Another is that he had the music box strapped to his leg under his pants. The third possible explanation is that spirits really *did* play the spectral music.

As for the bell that rang itself when set under the table, Houdini demonstrated this trick. A photograph in one of his books shows him doing it under the exact conditions attributed to Home. Houdini was seated at a séance table. Both of his hands were in plain view on top of the table. His feet were on the floor. A person on each side of him had placed a foot on top of his shoes to ensure that he did not use his feet. The small hand bell was placed on the floor under the table. The lights were extinguished. The bell was rung.

Houdini's hands and feet could not have been used. The witnesses were ready to swear that. So how did he do it?

He had placed metal shields in the toes of his shoes. These are just like the protective devices used in today's industrial safety shoes. The shoes were a loose fit. When the lights went out and after his guards had placed their feet on his to check any movement, Houdini slipped one foot from a shoe. The metal toe guard kept the weight of the guardian foot of the witness from depressing the empty shoe and revealing that Houdini's foot had been withdrawn.

The photograph shows that the toe of his sock had been cut away to leave his toes free. He picked up the bell between his toes, rang it vigorously, set it down, and slipped his foot back into the shoe unnoticed.

In the same manner he placed a sprig of flowers in the hand of a witness, just as it occurred at the Broome séance. Broome said he felt a ghostly thumb. Try pressing your thumb and then your big toe in the hand of a blindfolded person and ask them which was which. You cannot tell.

Levitation we have discussed. However, holding up one's shoes and letting someone touch them in the dark explains some of the floating tricks. It certainly does not explain the famous example at Lord Lindsay's home, when Daniel allegedly floated out one window and back in another.

We have told how Houdini promised to perform this feat *under the exact conditions imposed upon Home*. He cancelled the demonstration when his assistant became ill. We infer from this that the assistant was probably supposed to lower some kind of rope or platform down from the roof. This in itself would have violated the conditions. Home never used an assistant, for fear of exposing his methods.

Then how did he float from window to window three stories from the ground? Home alone knew the secret, and he took it to the grave with him. However, if I had to do the trick and could not get a platform outside, this is what I would *try* to do:

This was a stag party and the wine flowed freely. After a séance that put his audience in the proper frame of mind, Home let it be known that he was going to attempt something different, unusual, and dangerous. He had his audience face the window in their room while he took a chair removed from them and went into a trance. This, we know, happened.

In having his audience face the window, this put the séance table with its candle light behind the backs of the men. Home got up from his chair, still in a trance, and went into the adjoining room. He left the door open. They could not see him in the dark, but they could hear his voice *telling* them he was going out the window. He could well have leaned out the window so his voice would seem to come from outside.

The following is a speculation. While his audience's attention was riveted on the window in front of them, Home could have slipped quickly back into the room. They would not have seen him. He could then have stood directly beside the light so that its illumination fell directly upon him. This would have caused his reflection to show in the glass of the partially open window in front of his audience.

Now it is an optical peculiarity of mirrors that their reflections appear to be as far *behind* the glass as the objects they reflect are in front of the glass. Thus, Home's reflection on the window glass appeared to be several feet out in space. Lord Adare said later that they saw Home outside their window.

You can get this effect in your own house at night. Stand in front of a large window with the room lights illuminating your body. If the background outside the window is dark, you will see a ghost image of yourself apparently standing as far on the other side of the glass as you are on this side of it.

This effect was used in a London stage play in the late 1870's and was known as Pepper's Ghost. It permitted an actor to fight a duel with a ghost the audience could see through. It created a sensation.

With the image showing outside the window, it was then only necessary for Home to misdirect the audience's attention from the window and to move in front of it, recalling their attention by slamming shut the partially open window. The illusion would be complete.

If it seems improbable that he could have moved about the room unseen, we can only say that this happens on the magician's stage all the time. It is all a matter of adroit misdirection. And if the wine flowed as freely as it did at most Victorian-period stag parties, the gentlemen were not seeing too clearly anyway.

Home's startling exhibitions of fire handling were very dramatic, as all such exhibitions are. However, they are very simply explained. Fire handling and fire walking are among the oldest of occult tricks and are performed by magicians both black and white. They are still seen today in the Orient and in the South Seas.

Many explanations have been given for fire handling. One is that the fire walker or fire handler uses a special preparation to render his skin temporarily impervious to heat. Sir William Crookes denied this in his report on Home's amazing exhibition. Sir William is contradicted by a number of people more familiar with the subject than he was.

One of these is Jasper Maskelyne, magician son of the famous Nevil Maskelyne and grandson of the more famous John Nevil Maskelyne. In his book, *White Magic,* Makelyne gives a formula for rendering the tongue insensible to heat so that the magician can lick red-hot pokers.

Another who disagreed with Crookes is Julien J. Proskauer, formerly a well-known American magician, who wrote the book *Spook Crooks,* an exposé of crooked mediums. Proskauer gives a somewhat different formula from Maskelyne that can also protect the skin from extreme heat for at least enough time to perform some apparently miraculous tricks. Proskauer gives still another preparation which he says can be soaked into the hair and dried. Then the hair can be inserted directly into flames without singeing.

It will be recalled that this is exactly what Home did on one occasion at a séance with Crookes. The audience saw him stoop and insert his hair into the flames. They later inspected his hair and could find no sign of singeing or a smell of burned hair.

The case for Daniel Home was made in the earlier part of this book through reports of those who saw him. This chapter has tried to present a possible case against him by giving examples of how he might possibly have fooled people. But again we must repeat John Mulholland's admonition that there is no guarantee that Home used any of these methods.

Those who care to believe that Home was a genuine medium will find plenty of famous names from kings to Thackeray and Elizabeth Barrett Browning to support him. Those who believe him to have been a charlatan can call upon the reports of equally famous people from Charles Dickens to Robert Browning to support their stand. But neither side can prove its beliefs.

As to the possibility of ghosts and spirits being able to communicate with the living, the following statement was made by William Crookes—a man who did as much as anyone to investigate the possibility scientifically. The statement was contained in a letter written in 1874 in answer to an earnest request for information by a woman friend:

> During the whole time [of his experiments] I have most earnestly desired to get the one proof you seek—the proof that the dead can return and communicate. I have never once had satisfactory proof. I have had hundreds of communications *professing* to come from deceased friends, but whenever I try to get proof that they are really the individuals they profess to be, they break down. Not one has been able to answer the necessary questions to prove identity; and the great problem of the future is to me as impenetrable a mystery as ever it was.

All I am satisfied of is that there exist invisible intelligent beings, who profess to be spirits of deceased people. But the proofs I require I have never yet had. . . .

As for Daniel Home, he may have been a fraud, like so many of the mediums of his time, but he was not a crook. The Lyon case was the only time he was ever accused of any act that appeared to be illegal or which took advantage of anyone financially. In this case it appears clear that the accusations made against him were caused by Mrs. Lyon's pique at not being received into society, as she had hoped.

If Daniel Dunglas Home was a true medium, he was the greatest who ever lived. If he was a fraud, he was also the greatest of them all, for he alone evaded all attempts to trap him. This is more than even the famous mystic charlatan Cagliostro could do.

BIBLIOGRAPHY

Browning, Elizabeth Barrett, *Letters*. New York: The Macmillan Company, 1898.

Burton, Jean, *Heyday of a Wizard*. New York: Alfred A. Knopf, 1944.

Crookes, William, *Researches into the Phenomena of Spiritualism*. London: J. Burns, 1874.

Doyle, Arthur Conan, *The History of Spiritualism*. New York: George H. Doran, 1926.

Ebon, Martin, *They Knew the Unknown*. New York: World Publishing Company, 1971.

Hardinge, Emma, *Modern American Spiritualism*. London: Privately printed, 1870.

Harper's Weekly, issue of September 12, 1857. New York: Harper and Brothers.

Home, D. D., *Incidents in My Life* (First Series). London: Longman, Green, Longman, Roberts and Green, 1863.

Home, Mme D. D., *D. D. Home: His Life and Mission*. London: Kegan Paul, 1888.

Houdini, Harry (Erich Weiss), *A Magician Among the Spirits*. New York, Harper and Brothers, 1924.

Lytton, the Earl of, *The Life of Edward Bulwer, First Lord Lytton*. London: Macmillan and Co., 1913.

Mulholland, John, *Beware Familiar Spirits*. New York: Charles Scribners' Sons, 1938.

Miller, Betty, *Robert Browning*. New York: Charles Scribners' Sons, 1953.

Wallace, Alfred Russel, *Miracles and Modern Spiritualism*. London: George Redway, 1896.

INDEX

	JB	39561
	H	
AUTHOR	Edmonds, I.G.	
TITLE	D.D. Home:the man who talked with ghosts	

DATE LOANED	BORROWER'S NAME	DATE RETURNED
JUN 22	Tinteo	JUN 29 '79
AUG 22 '79	Steinka	5 '79
OCT 1 '84	Maryam Diel